Austrian Economics

Austrian Economics

An Introduction

Steven Horwitz

CATO INSTITUTE
WASHINGTON, DC

Print ISBN: 978-1-948647-95-3
eBook ISBN: 978-1-948647-96-0

Library of Congress Cataloging-in-Publication Data available.

Printed in the United States of America.

CATO INSTITUTE
1000 Massachusetts Avenue, NW
Washington, DC 20001
www.cato.org

CONTENTS

1

Introduction

The Austrian School of economics has received renewed attention in the past few decades as its free-market policy conclusions and association with libertarianism have played a growing role in academic and public debate. This attention became even greater during the housing crisis and the Great Recession, as Austrian ideas were frequently invoked to explain that boom-and-bust cycle. In addition, Ron Paul's campaigns for president in 2008 and 2012 made some of the school's ideas part of the popular political discourse. During the past decade, more young people have been studying the Austrian School as part of their formal college educations, because more economists with PhDs have been trained in that tradition and are themselves teaching at colleges and universities and contributing as public intellectuals to various media outlets.

The increasing public presence of the ideas of the Austrian School might suggest that this approach to economics is something new. However, the truth is otherwise. The Austrian School dates back to the revolution in economic thinking of the 1870s that created the modern approach to economics. At the turn of the 20th century, and for the next few decades, the Austrian School was one of the dominant schools of thought in economics. Its influence was diminished in the 1930s by two developments. First, the Keynesian revolution in macroeconomics that emerged out of the Great Depression pushed Austrian ideas aside. Around the same time, microeconomics was becoming increasingly expressed in formal mathematical terms, with economic problems being seen as special types of engineering problems. Both of these changes in the way economics was done were at odds with the Austrian approach. As a result, the Austrian School all but disappeared from around World War II until the early 1970s.

A second confluence of events, this time in the early 1970s, produced the conditions that led to a revival in the school's intellectual activity and reputation. The combination of high unemployment and high inflation in the early 1970s was not supposed to be possible according to the (broadly) Keynesian economic models in vogue at the time. The failure of mainstream macroeconomics to explain what was happening opened the door to alternative approaches. Two events in 1974, specifically, helped bring the Austrians back into the conversation. First was the awarding of the Nobel Prize in Economics to Friedrich August Hayek for his work on monetary theory and macroeconomics, as well as for his contributions to understanding the informational properties of the price system. All of this work was in the Austrian tradition. Also that year, the Harvard philosopher Robert Nozick published his National Book Award–winning *Anarchy, State, and Utopia*, a defense of libertarian political philosophy informed by ideas from the Austrian School.[1] Hayek's Nobel and Nozick's book put discussions of Austrian economics back on the agenda of scholars in a variety of disciplines, in addition to informing public debate.

These events, along with the publication of Israel Kirzner's *Competition and Entrepreneurship* the year before, marked the beginning of a revival of the Austrian School that has continued since, accelerating in the past decade thanks to the inability of the economics discipline to predict and explain the Great Recession.[2] Since the 1970s, the Austrian School has slowly elbowed its way into conversations in the mainstream of economics and is now informing policy analysis and public debate in ways it has not before. Although no reliable data exist, it is almost certain that there have never been more professional economists working in the Austrian tradition than there are today.

The Austrian School's roots are in the "Marginal Revolution" in economics that took place in the 1870s. That revolution fundamentally changed the way economists understood the concept of value, which had major consequences for the subject matter and methods of the discipline. Before the 1870s, the value of a good or service was most often explained with reference to the cost of producing it, especially the labor involved in doing so. The "labor theory of value" was, in one form or another, accepted by almost all major economic thinkers, from Adam Smith to Karl Marx. The theory has a number of obvious problems, including how to reduce different qualities of labor to a single measure and how to explain the value of things that are discovered serendipitously. Early economists worked hard to try to explain their way around these puzzles, much like Ptolemy resorted to inelegant mathematical contrivances to make his geocentric model of the solar system predictively accurate. The ad hoc nature of those explanations created the opportunity for a new systematic explanation of value, which arrived in the form of the Marginal Revolution, the economic equivalent of the Copernican Revolution in astronomy.

In the early 1870s, three thinkers changed the way economics was done by making clear that the value of a good or service was the result of the subjective perceptions of the usefulness to the consumer of the specific amount required for the use at hand (what is known as the "marginal" amount). Goods did not have intrinsic value, nor were their values determined by the amount of labor or other inputs that had gone into producing them. Instead, goods had value because people thought they were useful, and the specific amount of value they had depended on the particular quantity that was needed to satisfy the user's specific want.

Two of those three revolutionaries, William Stanley Jevons in England and Léon Walras in Switzerland, employed a mathematical approach, applying the concept of "marginality" to model their new conception of utility in terms of simple calculus. By contrast, the third of the three revolutionaries laid out a different understanding of this way of seeing value, stressing more than the other two the subjectivity of economic value and that the "margin" of choice was determined by the minds of those making choices rather than being an abstract mathematical concept. That third revolutionary was Carl Menger, a professor at the University of Vienna, and the approach to economics he laid out in his *Principles of Economics* in 1871 became the foundation of what was later termed the "Austrian School." In addition to his emphasis on the subjective nature of value, at the center of Menger's economics was human knowledge and the way in which its limits mean that we must constantly deal with uncertainty. For Menger, economics was the study of how humans possessing limited knowledge and facing an uncertain future attempted to improve their well-being by figuring out what they wanted and how best to get it. Menger's vision of economics was very much a human-centered one: "man, with his needs and his command of the means to satisfy them, is himself the point at which human economic life both begins and ends."[3] This conception of economics remains at the core of the modern Austrian School.

Menger's other great contribution was to expand and extend the "invisible hand" concept of Adam Smith. Both in his *Principles of Economics* and in his later book *Investigations into the Methods of the Social Sciences* (1883), Menger offered explanations of social phenomena that began with the choices of individuals and showed how the outcome of those choices was often a result that none of the individuals had planned or intended. In his *Principles*, he explained the emergence of money using this sort of strategy, and in the *Investigations*, he generalized that strategy and asked what is sometimes called the "Mengerian question":

> How can it be that institutions which serve the common welfare and are extremely significant for its development come into being without a common will directed toward establishing them?[4]

This explanatory strategy, later termed "spontaneous order theory," is also at the heart of modern Austrian economics. Understanding how social phenomena are the unintended outcomes of human choice filtered through various social institutions is the analytical technique Austrians use to do economics and social science. Spontaneous order explanations rest on the concepts of subjectivism and limited knowledge noted earlier. It is precisely because our knowledge is partial and local that we rely on social institutions, rather than the intelligent design and control of experts, to coordinate our behavior. This claim has broad implications for issues in political economy as well as for the nature of economics as a discipline.

In what follows, I will explore the ideas of the Austrian School of economics, with an emphasis on how its analysis differs from the standard textbook presentation of economics. My approach will be broadly historical, in that I will discuss specific ideas in roughly the historical order in which they became a focus of the school's attention. I will also not dwell on particular thinkers or books, but instead proceed topically and make note of important contributors as they are relevant to the ideas under consideration. Compared to the mainstream economics of today, the Austrian emphasis on subjectivism, uncertainty, and the importance of knowledge, as well as the school's conception of the market as a spontaneously ordered process of discovery, offers a different and more realistic explanation of economic phenomena, from the most basic to the most complex. As economics has become more abstract and more dependent on unrealistic assumptions about what humans know and how they choose, an approach that addresses those issues will find a receptive audience, as the revival of the Austrian School demonstrates.

2

Carl Menger and the Microeconomics of the Austrian School

In addition to the problems with the labor theory of value, the economists of the 18th century could not explain away what was known as the water-diamond paradox: water, which was essential for human life, was very cheap, but diamonds, which were a frivolous luxury, were very expensive. If it was admitted that the utility of goods somehow mattered for their value, then how was it possible that diamonds were more valuable than water, given how important water is for human survival? It was this puzzle that the Marginal Revolution solved. What mattered for value was not the *total utility* of a good (i.e., how much it is valued compared to its complete absence) but rather its *marginal utility*, or the value of the particular portion of the whole supply of the good that was consumed at any time. The value of a gallon of water is small because most people don't have a pressing need for one *additional* gallon. By contrast, a carat of diamonds has a high value, because the *marginal unit* is in high demand. This idea that the marginal unit determines the value of a good not only resolved the water-diamond paradox but also provided a new path forward for economics to understand value and price.

Unlike Jevons and Walras, in whose hands the distinction between total and marginal utility was quickly translated into mathematical terms, Menger combined the idea of "value on the margin" with his emphasis on subjectivism to offer a different approach to understanding economic processes. Menger started by noting that individuals want to satisfy particular ends (or "needs," as he referred to them). To do so, we require means at our disposal that are capable of satisfying those ends. This insight led Menger to define "goods" as things that have the capacity to satisfy some human want. That capacity is a good's *utility*. More specifically, he defined "economic goods" as those things capable of satisfying some end for which the quantity available is not sufficient to fulfill all the ends to which people might put them. "Non-economic goods," by contrast, are abundant enough that there is more than enough to satisfy all possible wants. Air, for example, satisfies our need to breathe, yet there is more than enough air for all of us to satisfy all of our breathing needs, unlike other products of nature or humanity, for which our wants exceed the quantity available.

At the center of Menger's theory of value was *subjectivism*. What gave a good its value was nothing inherent or intrinsic in the good itself, but rather the perception by humans that the good could be used to satisfy a want. My belief that I require a hammer to help build a house is sufficient to give that hammer value. (Whether there are more or fewer hammers available than wants they can satisfy will determine whether hammers are economic or non-economic goods.) The ultimate source of value is the human mind. Because our perceptions of what we require to satisfy our wants will be based on the specific quantity of the good we require, Menger's subjectivism was able to incorporate the idea of the margin. Whenever we evaluate the usefulness of a means to satisfy a want, we are thinking in terms of the particular, concrete amount of that good we wish to obtain.

Modern Austrian economics likes to stress one particular implication of Menger's framework. Too often, the idea of "utility" is explained as a kind of feeling we get from satisfying wants—when we make a sandwich for lunch and eat it, we get utility from the sandwich because it makes us feel good to satisfy that want. Aside from the fairly obvious point that something like dental work might satisfy a want but not "feel good," there is a deeper problem with this standard explanation. The Austrian conception of utility is not about a feeling people get. In the language of psychology, it is not "hedonic." Instead, it is the capacity of a good to satisfy a want. The "utility" of that sandwich is not the feeling it gives you but the fact that you believe it can address your desire to reduce your hunger. From this perspective, the marginal utility of a good is the ability of a specific, concrete amount of a good to satisfy the next most important unsatisfied want.

We can illustrate a number of Austrian insights with the following scenario. Imagine I have four wants I'd like to satisfy, each of which requires a gallon of water. Menger argued that people try to satisfy their most urgent wants first, followed by the less urgent wants in order of priority. What he called "economizing" was our attempt to take the means at our disposal and allocate them to the most urgent wants possible. Therefore, I will rank my four wants from most important to least and satisfy the most urgent want with the first gallon of water I can obtain, the next most urgent with the second, and so forth. If I can only obtain three gallons, the least urgent want will go unsatisfied. Let's see how this example can illustrate some key concepts.

First, water in general has utility because I believe it will help me satisfy those wants. My selection of which wants to satisfy, my ordering of their importance, and my decision to use gallons of water to satisfy them are all aspects of the subjectivism of Austrian economics. The fact that each want requires a specific amount of water to be satisfied lets us see the importance of the margin. My determination of how much value water has for me will depend on how I evaluate the importance of the gallon I am currently considering obtaining. And the importance of that gallon of water will in turn depend on the importance I attach to the want it will satisfy. That importance is not happiness or any other hedonic feeling—it is just the importance I associate with satisfying that want. Thus, the value of any good to an individual depends on the importance she attaches to the want that the marginal unit of that good will satisfy. If the gallon of water in front of me allows me to wash my car, then the value of that water is linked to the importance I place on my car being clean.

This example also lets us see how Austrians understand the core economic concepts of "opportunity cost" and "diminishing marginal utility." Opportunity cost is conventionally defined as the next best alternative given up when making a choice. We face scarcity, and choosing one thing means we give up the next best thing we could have chosen. Our gallons of water example illustrates this idea nicely. If we have three gallons of water, what is our opportunity cost of using up all three gallons? It's the want that goes unsatisfied after we do so.

Suppose the third most valued use was to water the garden and the fourth was to wash windows. Conventional economics would say that the opportunity cost of watering the garden is washing the windows. True enough, but the Austrian perspective adds two important elements: First, that opportunity cost is subjective. Only the chooser knows exactly the importance she attaches to watering the garden versus washing the windows. In this way, her opportunity cost cannot be objectively measured. Second, but more fundamentally, opportunity cost is never actually experienced, because it is the choice we did not make. Opportunity cost is ultimately her *expectation* of the importance of the sacrificed option. The very fact that she chose to water the garden means she never did wash the windows and thus never experienced just how important satisfying that want would actually be. When we choose, we choose among the subjective expected utilities of our different options. The option we evaluate to be the most important of those not chosen is not experienced. If I choose to order lobster macaroni and cheese rather than fish tacos, my opportunity cost is the subjectively expected utility I thought fish tacos would bring. I can never know with certainty what my opportunity cost was ex post, because I never experience the choice I didn't make.[5]

The idea of diminishing marginal utility looks different from this perspective as well. Normally, this concept is presented as the idea that the more you consume of a good, the less "good feeling" you get from it. So, while the first piece of cake might taste great, eventually successive pieces will taste worse and worse. But this explanation treats utility as hedonic, not as the capacity to satisfy a want. In our gallons of water example, the marginal utility of water is the importance attached to each gallon in relationship to its ability to satisfy a specific want. The first gallon enables us to wash the car, which is our most important want. The next gallon might be for drinking, our next most important want, followed by watering the garden and washing the windows. The marginal utility of each gallon is less than that of the previous one, because the importance we attach to the want it satisfies declines. Although we can say that marginal utility always declines as we obtain successive units of a good, we cannot put a number on that utility, because it remains subjective and expected.

Menger extended his discussion of goods, utility, and value to the process of production. According to the labor theory of value, it was the value of the inputs into a production process that determined how valuable the output of that process would be. The more labor that went into making a good, either directly or in the form of previously produced goods, the more valuable the good was. Menger turned that argument on its head and so completed the economics version of the Copernican Revolution. He first distinguished what he called "lower order" goods from "higher order" goods. The former are consumer goods, or things close to them: for example, the breakfast cereal on the shelf is a "first order" good. Higher order goods are the inputs that go into making lower order goods, such as the grains and sugar that go into making the cereal. Menger noted that what made a specific good higher or lower order was not any intrinsic property of the good but rather how that good fit into the plans of producers and consumers. For example, flour is a higher order good in the production of the cookies I buy at the store. But flour is a lower order good when it sits on the supermarket shelf for me to buy it to bake cookies at home. This conceptual framework allowed Menger, and the Austrian School in the years since, to talk about the "structure of capital" that produces the goods consumers buy.[6]

What Menger then argued was that value flowed not from the inputs to the outputs but from the outputs to the inputs. It was because those outputs were valued by consumers that the inputs that went into making them had value. So, because consumers like Big Macs, the two all-beef patties, special sauce, cheese, etc., and the labor of the employees who make them, have value. If people stopped eating beef, all of the factors of production that go into making Big Macs would lose some value. It is not labor that makes goods valuable, but rather people's belief that certain goods will satisfy their wants that gives value to the labor and materials that go into producing them. The ultimate source of value remains the subjective preferences and knowledge of each of us as consumers. Notice too that this transference of value from outputs to inputs is not automatic. Someone has to figure out (a) that people value some goods and not others and (b) which inputs are the best ones to make the outputs people value. That is the role of the entrepreneur, which we will discuss in more detail in Chapter 9.

This framework also helps us understand the distinctive twist Austrian economics puts on traditional supply and demand. In our discussion above, we left out money and exchange and just assumed that people either had, or would somehow acquire, goods like the gallons of water. In reality, of course, the choice facing consumers is whether to spend their money on one thing or another. In deciding whether to buy a gallon of water for $2, the consumer is really choosing between the expected subjective utility of using that gallon of water for the next most important want it could satisfy and the expected subjective utility of the most urgent unsatisfied want that the $2 could satisfy through the purchase of some other good. The ability to use money to buy any good means that we implicitly rank the expected subjective utilities of all of the alternative wants we might satisfy with a given amount of money. As we will see later, the existence of prices helps us navigate what would otherwise be an incredibly complex set of choices.

We can use this money-enhanced framework to offer an Austrian explanation for why people increase their quantity demanded of a good as its price falls. Consider our gallons of water example.[7] Your willingness to purchase more or fewer gallons of water to satisfy some or all of those four wants will depend on your comparison of the price for a gallon of water with the importance you attach to getting each of the wants satisfied. For example, you might be willing to pay $3 for a gallon to wash your car, but not to satisfy your thirst. If the price were $2.50, you'd still be willing to pay that price for a gallon to wash your car, and perhaps you'd also be willing to pay that price to satisfy your thirst. As the price falls further, your third- and fourth-ranked wants might become worth satisfying. The lower the price, the more willing people are to satisfy lower-ranked wants, because we have to give up less to do so. And if the price rose to $4, you might decide it's not worth it to wash your car, or satisfy any of the lesser-ranked ends, at that price. The demand curve is a reflection of diminishing marginal utility: the declining importance of the additional wants we have implies that what we are willing to sacrifice to satisfy those wants must be progressively less as we satisfy the less important ones. At higher prices, we will look for more important wants to satisfy. When prices fall, we are more willing to satisfy lower-ranked ends because we give up less to do so. Thus, we get downward-sloping demand curves: as prices fall, people wish to buy more units of a good, and as prices rise, they wish to buy fewer.

The same argument applies in reverse for supply curves. Suppose I have four gallons of water. To convince me to part with one of them will not take much, because that gallon is being used for the least important want, washing the windows. Since I don't value that end very highly, it won't take much to get me to give it up. But if you want me also to give up watering my garden by selling you two gallons of water, the price will have to be higher, because the importance of the next (marginal) want I would be unable to satisfy is greater.

So as the price of a good rises, people will increase the quantity of the good they supply, because at progressively higher prices they are more likely to be willing to give up satisfying more important wants by parting with that good. Higher prices mean a greater quantity supplied, and lower prices mean a lesser quantity supplied.

Finally, notice that supply here is just demand in disguise. I am more willing to part with additional gallons of water as I am offered more money in return, money I can use to satisfy more important wants than the water-related want I'm giving up. The amount of money I can get for my water is in turn determined by other people's demand for water—they are saying that their unsatisfied wants that require water are important enough for them to try to bid water away from me. The more important those ends are to them, the more they will be willing to pay to fulfill them. Humans attempting to acquire the means they believe will satisfy the wants they perceive to be important is where all of economics begins.

Market Process and Spontaneous Order

The other foundational part of Menger's work was his conception of the market as a process and the related concept that is now termed "spontaneous order." As noted earlier, the other two marginal revolutionaries, Jevons and Walras, formulated their versions of the theory in mathematical terms. Their work lent itself to seeing the task of economics as solving a static mathematical problem of how to allocate resources optimally. Marginalism became a way to set up the optimization problem, and economics became focused on describing those optimal equilibrium states and how changes to the system would change the resulting equilibrium. Often called "comparative statics," this approach to economics was like examining the differences between two still pictures of the economy. Menger, by contrast, offered something more like a moving picture, with the task of economics being to explain the *processes* by which economic change took place.

One way to see this different emphasis is in the organization of Menger's *Principles*. He begins with the definition of a "good" and his explanation of subjective value, then moves on to talk about the nature of exchange, then eventually gives his analysis of how prices come about. The structure indicates that prices are the emergent outcome of all of those underlying processes of subjective evaluation and exchange. By contrast, the Jevonian and Walrasian approaches, and their modern-day descendants of "partial equilibrium" and "general equilibrium" theory, respectively, *begin* with prices and then see what actors wish to demand or supply based on those prices. The goal of those approaches is to find the set of prices and quantities at which everyone is able to maximize their utility and profit, given the choices of others. Menger was more interested in explaining how the purposive actions of individuals would interact with each other through an ongoing process in real time to produce the particular prices and quantities we see at any given moment. Those need not be equilibrium prices and quantities, nor did Menger believe that the only interesting results to look for were those that involved maximization of utility and profits across the board. In fact, he did not even use the mathematical language of "maximization," because he recognized that humans were *imperfect* choosers acting on the basis of *limited* knowledge.[8]

This difference between process and equilibrium is at the heart of the modern Austrian School. Most economists today spend their time describing the properties of various equilibrium states and comparing the efficiency of those results. The economy is modeled as a system in equilibrium. The assumptions required for a real-world economy to be in equilibrium are very stringent. Equilibrium models in mainstream economics must assume, for example, that everyone possesses perfect relevant information, that no one can affect the price the market gives for a particular good, and that all goods of a certain type (e.g., breakfast cereals) are identical. Of course, the real world is one of imperfect information and uncertainty, where some sellers and buyers have more influence than others, and where products are differentiated along any number of dimensions. Austrians see the market as a process by which partially informed people learn from each other and discover what it is that others want and how best to produce it.

The key to this learning process is the entrepreneur. We will explore the role of the entrepreneur in more depth in a later chapter, but for now, it suffices to say that the entrepreneur is the one who pushes forward the learning process of the market by being alert to opportunities that current market participants have overlooked. If apples are selling for $2 per pound on one side of the street and $3 per pound on the other, some buyers have overlooked cheaper apples and some sellers have overlooked a better selling opportunity. This disequilibrium reflects the limited knowledge of buyers and sellers. An entrepreneur who spots this situation can buy up the apples on the one side for, say, $2.25 per pound and sell them on the other side for somewhere between $2.25 per pound and $3 per pound. This entrepreneurial act informs both groups of their errors and helps correct them by reducing or eliminating the price discrepancy. When entrepreneurs do this, they benefit all parties. The people selling at $2 per pound get a higher price, the people buying at $3 per pound get a lower price, and the entrepreneur profits. Viewed in isolation, entrepreneurship also brings the market closer to the hypothesized equilibrium by narrowing the range of prices available until, in the limit, the market has just one price for apples and the number of apples offered at that price exactly equals the number people desire to purchase.

The Austrian concern with the market process enables us to recognize that the limit point never comes, because the factors that define the point of equilibrium never stay constant. People's preferences change, the cost of producing goods changes, or the available substitutes might change, any of which changes the optimum point. Austrians are interested in how those changes take place and how actors, especially entrepreneurs, learn from and respond to them. One implication of this perspective is that it is very difficult to look at a market at any one point in time and know how well it is performing. Any snapshot fails to realize that markets are always in a state of transition as human knowledge changes. The effectiveness of a market is not about how it compares to an ideal at any point in time but how easily people can learn from their mistakes and have incentives to correct them. Because real-world markets never actually settle into a final equilibrium, we are always evaluating the performance of the market in terms of the way in which disequilibrium prices serve to provide the knowledge and incentives people need to better coordinate their plans. We will examine this argument in more detail later when we discuss the role of prices. Understanding this point requires the emphasis on the market process that began with Menger.

Menger's work also gave Austrian economics a second part of its distinct identity. As Chapter 1 noted, both in his *Principles* and then in his *Investigations*, Menger sought to explain how social outcomes emerged without human beings intentionally designing them. In the *Principles*, the major example of this type of process was Menger's famous explanation of the origin of money.[9] He argued that no one invented money; instead, it emerged unplanned out of people's attempts to improve their want-satisfaction through exchange.

Imagine a barter economy, in which the only way trade can happen is if someone else both has what you want *and wants what you have*. The need to find this "double coincidence of wants" makes only a few exchanges possible.

However, some goods will be more sought after in exchange. Menger notes that which goods these will be would depend on the various subjective evaluations of consumers. Some traders will notice that those goods are more popular and will attempt to acquire stocks of those goods—not because they value the goods for direct consumption, but because they believe the goods can be easily exchanged for other goods they do wish to consume. This is the process of "indirect exchange." All of those intermediary goods can be called "mediums of exchange," but they are not yet money. Menger argued that other traders would observe the ease with which users of those intermediary goods could make exchanges and would start to imitate them. This, of course, would make the intermediary goods even more in demand and therefore more valuable as media of exchange. Eventually, some very small number of goods win out as the most easily exchanged, usually just one or two. These goods are truly money, because they are *generally accepted mediums of exchange.* For something to be a money, it has to be more than just something used as a medium of exchange. People have to believe, correctly, that it will be accepted routinely, in a way they need not think about. Once money exists, exchanges become much easier, and people can more easily increase their wealth and want-satisfaction.

Menger's theory of money's origin is the quintessential example of what Hayek and others would later term a "spontaneous order." None of the actors making exchanges is intending to create a new social institution. Each is simply trying to improve his or her own situation by exchanging to better satisfy their wants. Nonetheless, they unintentionally bring about a highly beneficial outcome by causing the emergence of money. The 18th-century Scottish moral philosopher Adam Ferguson offered a short definition of spontaneous orders (such as money), calling them "the results of human action, but not of human design."[10] This idea of spontaneous order is a core analytical concept for the Austrian School. Ferguson was a contemporary of Adam Smith, and one way to view Menger's contributions to social analysis is that he was developing and expanding on Smith's concept of the "invisible hand." Smith is usually credited as being the first modern economist, because he recognized the way in which market economies exhibited order without design. He understood that the right set of social institutions could harness broadly self-interested behavior to unintentionally serve the needs of others. When we are "led by an invisible hand to promote an end which was no part of [our] intention," it is because institutions provide us with the information and incentives we need to know how best to create value for others.[11] In *The Wealth of Nations*, Smith was the first to articulate this idea in a clear way and then apply it to economic activity.

Menger's theory of money and his broader elucidation of the idea of spontaneous order in his *Investigations into the Methods of the Social Sciences* advanced Smith's work by more carefully identifying the process by which social institutions emerged without design and by placing that process at the center of the social sciences. By combining spontaneous order with marginalism and subjectivism, Menger provided a more solid microeconomic foundation for Smith's insight. In arguing that prices were themselves an example of order without design that had emerged from the subjective and marginal evaluations of traders, Menger opened the door to the Austrian conception of prices as knowledge surrogates that would become more prominent in Hayek's work in the 20th century. From explaining how particular prices emerge, to the more general patterns of economic outcomes, to the emergence and function of large-scale social institutions, Austrians start with the perceptions and actions of individuals and show how they interact to produce outcomes that none of them intended or designed. Understanding that much of the world around us is not something humans consciously created has numerous implications for particular aspects of economics, as we will see in later chapters.

Spontaneous order theory has also pointed Austrians toward the importance of social institutions in ensuring that self-interested action leads to social benefits. What makes the invisible hand work, or puts the "order" in spontaneous order, is having the right set of social and economic institutions to provide the feedback and incentives necessary to properly channel self-interest toward benefiting others. For example, where property rights are clearly defined and well enforced, production and exchange are more likely, and market prices will be better reflectors of value. The search for profit will lead entrepreneurs to provide the goods and services that others want. Where property rights are not as clear, or where public policy distorts the costs facing entrepreneurs, the self-interested search for profit will not produce the same level of benefits to the public. The invisible hand generates good outcomes when the rules of the game are able to provide the needed feedback and incentives. The efficacy of economic processes is not, according to the Austrians, the result of the behavior of individuals nearly as much as it is of having the right institutions for those individuals to act under. Economic progress comes not from the pursuit of self-interest or from rational choice, per se, but from having the right structure in which to take those actions. Providing Smith's invisible hand insight with a clearer foundation in economics broadened our understanding of spontaneous orders and gave the Austrians an important analytical tool for understanding economic and social processes.[12]

4

The Method of Austrian Economics

Menger's theory of the origin of money and his broader work on spontaneous order also offer a template for the way economics as a discipline should proceed. The Austrian School economist Ludwig von Mises wrote in *Human Action* that, in developing his theory of money, Menger "also recognized the import of his theory for the elucidation of fundamental principles of praxeology and its methods of research."[13] Mises elaborates by using the theory as an example of methodological individualism and of how historical contingencies will affect the precise way in which economic processes unfold *without* contradicting the core laws of economics. What Mises called "praxeology" in *Human Action* in the mid-20th century was another name for what he saw as the way good economics had always been done: studying human action and its consequences, both intended and unintended. For Mises, there was a core of economic theory that was both irrefutable and necessary for any sort of applied, empirical, or historical research. The claim that economics must include a deductive component that provides the theory through which we then look at the world is a claim that goes back to Menger and the origins of Austrian economics.

Menger's *Principles of Economics* was dedicated to Wilhelm Roscher, the leading thinker of the German Historical School. That school of thought held that the proper method of economics was to do historical studies and understand particular economies in their own contexts. They were skeptical of the sort of universal theory espoused by the classical economists. Menger learned this tradition, and he saw his book as a contribution to it because he believed his theoretical framework would enhance historical understanding. One can see his explanation of money's origin as an example of what he thought could be done. He was not rejecting the doing of history as an important task for economists—he simply thought it could be done much better with an explicit theory of the sort he was developing.

Because of the criticism of the *Principles* by the German Historical School, Menger proceeded to expand on these themes in 1883 in his *Investigations*. There he distinguishes between "exact laws" and "realist-empirical generalizations." The former are the sorts of "if-then" statements that we usually associate with economic theory today. For example, "if all else is held equal, then an increase in the price of a good will lower its quantity demanded." The latter are statements of empirical regularities, such as the argument that the boom of a business cycle usually involves an increase in lending to producers rather than consumers. These sorts of statements are not necessary truths, just frequently observed empirical tendencies. Menger's distinction fairly closely corresponds to the way Mises would later distinguish theory from history. In particular, Menger is clear to say that "exact laws" are not tested by history, although he, like Mises, distinguishes the *validity* of a particular piece of theory from the question of whether it *applies* in any specific historical circumstance.[14]

Menger's defense of the existence and importance of pure theory, and his argument that one could not engage in effective historical work without it, threw down the gauntlet in front of the German Historical School. The leader of the younger generation of that school, Gustav Schmoller, responded by sharply accusing Menger of merely extending the arid theory-building of the classical economists, with little interest in understanding the real world. The original exchange between Schmoller and Menger began what is now known as the *methodenstreit*, or "battle of methods," between the two schools. Several further exchanges took place as Menger attempted to defend the role of theory and Schmoller and his colleagues continued to argue for a historically-based economics. Modern economists largely see this debate as a waste of time, because they generally agree that there is an important role for theory but that theory has to be tested against the real world. They see the Austrians and the Historical School as talking past each other and not realizing that the truth was elsewhere.[15]

The Austrians, however, continued to insist on an understanding of theory that strongly differentiated it from history and that saw the core of economic theory as being known a priori and therefore untestable empirically.[16] In the 20th century, Ludwig von Mises expanded on this idea by distinguishing between the a priori truths of the core of economic theory and what we learn about particular events when we apply those economic laws along with contingent facts about particular institutions and policies. Modern Austrians today see economic theory as a pair of eyeglasses that are necessary to understand cause and effect in the economic and social world. This leads many Austrian School economists to see only limited value in econometric studies, particularly if such studies suggest their empirical findings can be universalized as if they were theory. Modern Austrians have tried to expand the range of empirical evidence that economists might rely on by including not just statistical data but also qualitative evidence such as interviews, surveys, and primary historical documents.

Mises spent an entire chapter of *Human Action* on "the scope and method of catallactics." Catallactics is Mises's term for the study of market exchange, what we today would broadly identify as economics. He saw catallactics as a subcategory of the overarching science of all human action, which he termed "praxeology." Humans engage in a variety of purposive actions that are not about exchange on the marketplace (e.g., the management of a household, including the raising of children, or the conduct of war, or the playing of games). Those actions are excluded from catallactics, or economics in the more narrow sense, but are still part of the broader category of praxeology.

In that chapter, Mises wrote that "the specific method of economics is the method of imaginary constructions." He went on to explain how each of these constructions is "a conceptual image of a sequence of events logically evolved from the elements of action employed in its formation." One can see this method at work in the way Austrian economists use supply and demand curves and the concept of equilibrium. These imaginary constructions are the products of logical deductions that start with the basic idea of purposive action, that humans seek to remove the "felt uneasiness" of unsatisfied ends by finding means effective for satisfying them. Mises argues that it is irrefutable that we act purposively and further argues that purposive action logically implies some important observations about human action that are just as "apodictically certain" as the claim that people act.[17]

There is much debate among Austrians about how extensive that logically-consequent set of apodictically certain claims is. Some Austrians argue as if one can deduce all of economics from one's armchair, but Mises was pretty clear that this core of economics is fairly limited. He points out that even the notion that labor is unpleasant is not part of that core, but rather an auxiliary assumption we make based on observation. So too is the existence of things like money. When the economist goes to analyze the world, the core toolkit that comes only from reflection on action is a rather small set of basic propositions. Most of the interesting work in economics is institutionally contingent. Moving from what Menger called "exact laws," or pure theory, to applied theory requires including the human beliefs and social institutions of the empirical world. Going from applied theory to economic history, including contemporary analyses, economists need to dig into the actual empirical record of what people did and thought as well as the relevant economic data.

This point is also related to what Mises means by saying economics is an a priori science. He is not claiming that Austrians reject any form of empirical analysis and believe that one can, for example, reach policy conclusions by just sitting in one's armchair. Instead, Mises is making a philosophical claim about the human mind and the way in which minds are similarly structured across humans. We all have a set of mental tools for grasping reality that comes to us from our evolutionary heritage. Any being with equivalent tools would be able to engage in reflection on the nature of human action and develop that core of economics as a set of necessary insights about how humans act. This core economic knowledge is not in any sense contingent; rather, it is part of the very structure of certain sorts of minds, including those of humans as we have evolved on Earth.

Mises did argue that these core claims of economics (e.g., that people act purposively, that we prefer more to less and now to later, the idea of diminishing marginal utility, and perhaps the basic idea behind demand and supply curves) are not open to empirical proof because they are the very organizing principles of our attempts to understand the world. However, beyond that, and especially if we are to include any claims about policy, economic arguments depend on contingent claims about human behavior and preferences, the applicability of our assumptions, and the accuracy of our chains of argument. Good economics for Austrians means *sound* arguments, not just valid ones. Too much of modern economics is valid reasoning from false premises about human action. The accuracy of those premises matters greatly for Austrians, and their accuracy can be a matter of empirical fact when we examine specific historical episodes.

Despite the pretensions of many mainstream economists, their empirical studies, including newer work in experimental economics, do not have quite the same scientific power as experiments in the natural sciences do. Stephen Ziliak and Deirdre McCloskey's cautions about the importance of statistical significance are on target but often ignored by economists. As they argue, what we want is *economic significance*, not just statistical significance.[18] Austrians would agree. For Austrians, the goal is to provide economic analyses that use empirical evidence that is economically significant. Achieving the goal of rendering human action intelligible means telling better stories about what happened and why.

Economic theory provides the framework for organizing the plot, and the richness of the human experience—whether in the form of primary sources, interview and survey data, economic statistics, or econometric correlations—provides the particulars that make for a complete and empirically-relevant story. Basing it all on realistic and empirically relevant assumptions about human knowledge and choice makes it not just valid but sound economic reasoning.

Modern Austrian economists recognize the importance of illustrating the power of economic theory by applying it to historical events, both recent and deeper in the past. Although this work in economic history does not "test" Austrian theory, it does show how the theory can help us better understand history, and it forces Austrians to clarify which parts of their theories are in that untestable core and which parts are institutionally or historically contingent. For example, the housing boom and financial crisis of the early 2000s can be made intelligible using the Austrian theory of the business cycle, but only if one recognizes that the theory proper cannot explain why the excess supply of credit was diverted to housing specifically. Understanding why this particular cyclical boom manifested in rising housing prices requires additional empirical facts that were contingent features of government policy over the past few decades. The theory helps us understand the history, and the history forces us to be more precise about what is actually part of the theory.

Over a century after the *methodenstreit*, Austrians have refined their understanding of the relationship between theory and history, but their major claims—that there is a core of economic theory that is a priori and untestable, that history cannot be done without such theory, and that history cannot give us definitive laws—remain central to the school's work.

5

Capital and Calculation

Modern Austrian economics conceives of the market as a competitive discovery process driven by monetary calculation. In market economies, producers must solve two problems: what is it that people wish to buy and how best to make those things such that the output is worth more than the inputs (if doing so is even possible). Solving these two problems involves the process of *monetary calculation*, which is the tallying up of past and prospective profit and loss.[19] For the Austrian School, monetary calculation is necessary to solve a problem that arises because of the flexible nature of capital goods. Austrians believe their theory of capital is indispensable for correctly understanding the way economic production can satisfy people's wants and needs.

For the moment, we can put aside the problem of figuring out what it is that consumers wish to buy. Even if we are able to know that information in the absence of market prices and profit and loss signals, we still must figure out how best to produce those goods. This aspect of the problem of economic calculation is often overlooked by people skeptical of markets. To the extent they realize that obtaining the knowledge necessary for production is a challenge for producers, they seem to think the relevant knowledge is just about consumer preferences. Such critics are often inclined to think that this problem could be solved through some sort of combination of survey instruments and networked computers. It can't, as we'll see in the next chapter. But even if it could, the second, and perhaps more difficult, problem of how best to produce those goods and services remains.

Any given output can be produced by a whole variety of methods and combinations of inputs. Which ones should producers choose? Suppose you could produce men's athletic shoes with several different materials, from leather to canvas to some form of plastic. Suppose further that there were various amounts of labor, and combinations of labor and inputs, that could be used to produce the shoes. Or suppose you knew people wanted leather shoes. How much of which kind of leather would you use? How much labor versus how many machines would you use? Answering these questions of how best to produce goods, even when you know more or less what people would like to buy, requires the ability to compare alternative production processes through monetary calculation with market prices.

Or consider the reverse: any given input can be used to make some number of outputs, which outputs should you make with it? You have a pile of 2×4 pieces of wood in front of you. They can contribute to a large number of possible outputs. Which production process should they be devoted to? How would you go about answering that question in the absence of market prices by which to compare the alternatives? The fundamental problem facing producers is that each output can be made with a large number of alternative production processes and that each input can be used to produce some number of alternative outputs. How to figure out which inputs to use to make which outputs is the challenge of production in any economy.

At the center of this problem is the nature of capital. All economists understand that capital is an input into the production process, along with labor, and modern economics even refers to labor (or, more specifically, the skills, knowledge, and experience of workers) as "human capital." However, when mainstream economists model production, they treat capital as an undifferentiated aggregate. Standard production models simply have a K (for capital) and an L (for labor) and are framed in terms of how much of each aggregate is needed to produce a particular output. By contrast, Austrians start by thinking of capital in terms of specific capital goods or specific human beings with particular skills. Specific capital goods can be used for more than one use, but not for *any* use.

It is this "multiple specificity" of capital that creates the need for monetary calculation.[20] If each capital good had one and only one use, the problem of how to use that good would be nonexistent. If capital goods were infinitely malleable and could be used to produce anything, which is essentially what mainstream models assume by treating capital as an aggregate K, then here too the problem of which production process gets which capital good essentially disappears. The problem of which inputs to use for which outputs matters because capital goods have this specificity. Once capital is viewed this way, the problem of production becomes not a problem of *how much* capital to use, as if capital could be ladled out like soup, but rather *which* capital to use such that the capital goods and human capital fit together in the right way to make the desired output. Rather than ladles of soup, Austrians see capital as being like pieces of a jigsaw puzzle.[21] Only certain pieces will fit together with other pieces in the right way to make the desired pattern. The goal is not to just use more pieces but to use the right pieces. Figuring out which pieces are the right ones and whether they fit together requires economic calculation.

This view of capital has been dominant in the Austrian School since Menger. Unlike the classical economists' cost-of-production theories of value, in which the value of the input determined the value of the output, subjectivism and marginalism show us that the reverse is true. The value of *inputs* derives from the value consumers place on the *outputs* they produce. Capital and labor and land have value because consumers value the goods those particular inputs help to produce. Resources flow from raw materials and other inputs to consumer goods, but value flows from consumer demands to inputs. Menger also recognized that capital goods can be described in terms of their proximity to the ultimate output.[22] So, for example, the bread that is part of the sandwich I buy at the deli is a first-order capital good, because it directly contributes to a consumer good. The wheat that goes into making that bread is a second-order capital good for making that sandwich, because it is an input into the first-order good. Note too that the very same physical good can be a first-order or a second-order good depending on the output in question. A bakery can buy flour to make bread that it sells to the deli to make sandwiches the deli will sell, or the bakery can use that same flour to bake a cake that it sells to a consumer. Flour is a second-order capital good for the sandwich but a first-order capital good for the cake. And if a consumer buys that same flour to use at home, it's a consumer good and not a capital good at all. What makes something capital in the first place is not its physical qualities but its role in the process of production.

Given all of these complexities, some way to sort out the alternatives is required. Here is where monetary calculation comes in. The fundamental fact of market economies is the exchange of money for goods and services. If we imagine a barter economy, in which people trade goods directly for goods, we can see one of the problems it would have: instead of a single price denominated in money, each good would have millions of different prices—one for each and every other good it trades for. Apples would have prices in terms of oranges, bananas, horses, automobiles, and everything else. If such a world were even possible, any attempt to compare the values of alternative combinations of inputs would get impossibly complex very quickly.

The use of money gives us a universal set of prices reckoned in terms of just one good. Now each good has a price, and all of those prices are in terms of the same good. Observing a price in money doesn't tell us a good's value in the way that observing a thermometer reading tells us something's temperature, but because money prices are causally related to the subjective valuations of goods by economic agents, money prices are an indispensable tool of comparison. With money prices, we can much more easily compare alternative combinations of inputs than we could by comparing everything in kind.

When we trade money for goods and services, we are part of the supply and demand process from which those prices emerge. In this way, those prices reflect our preferences and subjective costs as well as those of all the other consumers and producers participating in the market. Those prices then feed into the decisionmaking process of firms as they figure out what people want and how best to produce it. By reducing all exchange ratios to a common denominator, monetary exchange allows prices to be consistent reflections of preferences and costs, and it thereby enables us to make calculations of profits and losses and to form budgets.

Budgets are the first step in this process of monetary calculation. Firms make their best guesses as to what their inputs will cost and how much revenue they can obtain for the final product. After the period being budgeted for has passed, the firm will know its profits or losses. Budgeting uses monetary calculations to try to make the best decisions possible before the fact about how to allocate inputs, and profits and losses tell producers after the fact just how good or bad their decisions were. Profits signal that value has been created; losses signal the destruction of value. What the process of monetary calculation does is enable us to determine which, among the various technologically possible ways of producing a good, is the most economically efficient—that is, which one creates the most value, as indicated by profit and loss.

This is also a process without end. Once profits or losses are figured for the last period, those data must be interpreted by the entrepreneur and a new budget must be formulated for the next period, which will then be tested again by profit and loss. In particular, the entrepreneur will have to decide what, if any, changes are necessary to the combination of capital goods and labor that was used in the most recent production process. Losses indicate that those inputs did not fit together as well as was expected, so pulling the combination apart and substituting new inputs may be necessary. This constant shuffling and reshuffling of capital combinations on the basis of the profit and loss data emerging from competition is the learning process of the market, made necessary by the multiple specificity of capital and addressed by the existence of prices, formed by monetary exchange, that enable us to engage in monetary calculation.

This Austrian perspective on capital and monetary calculation gives us a somewhat different take on profit and loss than one would typically see in a mainstream economics textbook. Most standard presentations focus on the *incentive* effects of profit and loss—we also see this matter discussed as the importance of the "profit motive." It is certainly true that profits (and losses) serve as an incentive or a motive for people to make good decisions about how to allocate resources. The lure of profit matters for getting people to think about how best to create value. However, motivation alone is not enough. Even if everyone deeply desired to create value for others, that motivation could not answer the question of *how* such value should be created. Without knowledge of how well or how poorly we are acting on our desires, our desires alone cannot get us to the socially desirable result. The key function of profit and loss from an Austrian perspective is not motivational but *epistemic*: profit and loss signals provide us with knowledge that we would otherwise lack. Seeing profit and loss this way also offers a different way of seeing policies like subsidies, bailouts, or confiscatory taxes on profit. All of those policies short-circuit the profit-and-loss process and thereby prevent it from sending accurate signals to (and providing the correct incentives for) entrepreneurs. Profit and loss are like the pleasure and pain signals sent by our nerve endings. If we didn't feel the pain of our hand on a hot stove, we wouldn't know that we were burning ourselves. Policies that distort the profit-and-loss process prevent us from knowing how well or how poorly we are making use of resources. Without genuine profit and loss signals, producers are flying blind, and consumers suffer as a result.

6

The Socialist Calculation Debate

The Austrian description of the way in which capital and monetary calculation drive the market process discussed in the previous chapter, was front and center in one of the most important social scientific debates of the 20th century. Starting with Karl Marx's work in the middle of the 19th century, numerous thinkers had developed arguments for the superiority of socialism and the central planning of economies. By the early 20th century, these arguments had combined with a strong faith in rationalism and science, and the experiences many countries had in centralizing their economies during World War I, to create a vision of socialism as substituting intentional, scientific economic management for the more haphazard learning process of capitalism. Socialism was to be preferred to capitalism not only because it was more just, by virtue of eliminating the exploitative capitalist class, but also because it would be more rational and efficient since it substituted before-the-fact economic planning for the wasteful learning-after-the-fact that characterized the profit and loss system of capitalism. Economic planners could, the socialists argued, gather the information necessary to decide what needed to be produced and how best to produce it—without the use of money, markets, or prices. By doing so, the socialists believed planners could avoid the waste associated with relying on competition to sort out the better and worse among the diverse plans of entrepreneurs.

Into the midst of the rising tide of socialism and economic planning stepped the Austrians, particularly Ludwig von Mises. In 1920, Mises published his essay "Economic Calculation in the Socialist Commonwealth," which he followed up with his book *Socialism* in 1922.[23] The central claim of the 1920 essay, which was also at the core of the book, was that socialist economic planning was *impossible*, in the sense that there was no way such planners could know whether any potential allocation of resources was more efficient than any other, no way for them to assemble any sort of rational plan. Therefore, socialism could *not* outproduce capitalism.

Mises's argument was that the rational allocation of resources requires some way of comparing the alternative processes of production and the outputs they produce. Mises considered and dismissed various methods of comparison on the basis of the labor involved in producing goods that a socialist central planner might employ, primarily because there was no abstract unit of labor into which labor could be reduced. Then Mises argued that only market prices can serve this purpose adequately. Such prices may not be perfect reflections of value, but they are sufficiently good to enable the relevant comparisons and are better than any alternative.

Mises did not stop there, however. He also argued that for prices to do this work, they had to be actual market prices that emerged from trading money for goods. It was the exchange against money, meaning that each good was being compared to the same single good (money), that produced a universal unit of account and allowed people to perform economic calculations. But for goods to trade against money, there had to be market exchange. Market exchange, Mises continued, required that there be private property. For Mises, having prices that were sufficiently meaningful to enable the required comparisons of value was only possible when such prices emerged from the exchange of private property for a commonly accepted medium of exchange in the market process. Mises emphasized that this was especially true of capital goods. Even if we could imagine an economy in which personal consumption goods were traded in markets or in which planners could know exactly what sorts of such goods people wanted, the question of how best to make those goods would remain.

As the previous chapter discussed, the problem in *any* economic system is how to determine both how to use goods that can be inputs into multiple processes of production and which of the many technologically feasible methods of making a particular good is the most economically efficient. What Mises pointed out in the early 1920s is that, whatever its imperfections, there is no way to answer that question without using market prices—assuming one cared about rational resource allocation, as the early socialists did. This included the need for market prices of capital goods. And if market prices could only emerge through the exchange of private property against money, then a world in which capital goods were commonly owned, as the socialists proposed, would be a world in which rational resource allocation was impossible. An advanced, complex, prosperous economy characterized by a high degree of social cooperation had to be a capitalist one, in that it had to have private ownership of the means of production. Mises claimed that his argument dealt a fatal blow to the claims of socialists that their system would be more productive and efficient than capitalism. Furthermore, the impossibility of socialist planning precluded any claim of socialism being more just.

Mises's challenge to the socialists was an application of the Austrian ideas raised in the previous chapter. Not only did the Austrian understandings of capital and monetary calculation describe how markets worked, they described why socialism couldn't. The way in which markets enable people to make use of the knowledge of others through the signals of prices, profits, and losses has its imperfections, as Mises noted in 1920, but there was no way, given the complexities involved with capital goods with multiple uses, that we could do without the "aids to the mind" that prices provided.[24] It is true that market competition involves waste, as seen from the present looking into the past, but that waste is a necessary byproduct of the same process that helps us get resource allocation as right as we often do. Learning after the fact through the signals of profit and loss is the only way to know whether we have created value, and so we cannot afford to abolish those signals by eliminating the private ownership of the means of production on which they rest. As desirable as it might be to know with certainty before we produced whether we were doing the right thing, this ability is not within the realm of human possibility, Mises argued. He believed this argument was a decisive refutation of the possibility of rational economic calculation under socialism.

During the 1920s and 1930s, several socialists and mainstream economists responded to Mises's argument, the most famous of whom was the Polish economist Oskar Lange. In 1936, Lange argued that standard economic theory gave no reason to think that state ownership of capital couldn't produce the optimal outcomes that the same theory said markets could.[25] More specifically, several of the so-called "market socialists" like Lange offered versions of the argument that a "Central Planning Board" (CPB) could use a trial-and-error method to determine the optimal allocation of capital goods. Mises, argued the market socialists, was mistaken to think that prices must be generated by the exchange of private property for money to be useful. The CPB could name a price and see how much of that input producers would demand and supply, then the CPB could reduce the price if there were a surplus and raise the price if there were a shortage. Lange and others believed that successive rounds of this process could generate the equilibrium prices of inputs that were necessary to assure efficient resource allocation. In their view, the CPB was simply playing the role of "the market" by providing prices as givens into the calculations of producers.

Lange argued that the planners required the same knowledge that was assumed by economists to be "given" when they used equilibrium theory to explain how markets work. If so, and if the trial and error method—which just mimicked the market anyway, they thought—could work, then there was no reason *on theoretical grounds* to think that planning and public ownership of the means of production could not produce rational resource allocation.

F. A. Hayek picked up the Austrian side of the debate, arguing that Lange and others had misunderstood the nature of markets, especially the ways in which they created unplanned order by enabling us to make use of each other's knowledge through monetary calculation and the price system.[26] Hayek suggested that economics had become too caught up in abstract modeling of equilibrium outcomes, which assumed away the key questions about knowledge that necessitated the existence of markets and monetary calculation. These equilibrium models gave economists the false belief that they could plan the unplannable. Hayek's alternative vision of the economy was one in which the price system allowed individuals to share knowledge that would otherwise be unknown and unusable—and thus impossible for economists or planners to acquire and use in large-scale economic plans. Hayek returned to Menger's theme of spontaneous order, now deepened by a new understanding of the role of prices as knowledge surrogates in a process of social learning.[27] (Chapter 8 has more on this point.)

With the hindsight of more than 75 years, we know that the Austrians had it right all along: socialist planning was impossible. The nature of human knowledge and the complexity of capital allocation make it impossible to manage economies from the top down rather than relying on a distributed decisionmaking process driven by the signals of prices and profits. Governments that attempted to do so quickly found themselves unable to achieve their desired ends of prosperity and greater economic equality. In country after country, rather than admit failure, socialist and communist governments further consolidated power, impoverishing their citizenry while political leaders enhanced their personal influence and material wealth. Almost all of the nominally socialist regimes collapsed by the end of the 20th century, vindicating Mises, Hayek, and the Austrians.

However, that was not the verdict in the 1940s. The economics profession generally sided with Lange and the market socialists, at least to the extent that economists agreed that there was no *theoretical* reason to prefer markets to planning. Lange showed, they argued, that theory could go either way and that we had to make such determinations case by case, depending on the particulars. The claim made by Mises and Hayek during the socialist calculation debate that socialist planning was impossible was rejected.

The debate was thought to be settled until the mid-1980s, when Don Lavoie published his book *Rivalry and Central Planning*, rekindling the debate and strengthening the Austrian case against socialist planning.[28] Lavoie reviewed the debate, focusing on the exchanges between Hayek and Lange. He argued that Lange, as well as the later economists who sided with him, had misunderstood the Austrian argument because he did not fully understand the Austrians' dynamic view of competition and their skepticism of equilibrium theory. Lavoie was able to more clearly articulate the Austrian view, thanks to decades of subsequent work in the Austrian tradition, and to demonstrate that Mises and Hayek had made a different and stronger argument than their critics had thought. Lavoie's timing was excellent, as by 1985, the failures of really-existing socialism were becoming clear, so that the Austrian case against planning was converging with the empirical evidence. His book forced a rethinking of the case for socialist planning and a broader reconsideration of the arguments against the Austrian School more broadly. Even Robert Heilbroner, a well-known historian of economic thought who was also a socialist, eventually conceded that "Mises was right."[29]

One of the ironies of the perception that the Austrians lost the calculation debate is that it, along with a similar perception of Hayek's defeat in his debate with Keynes (see Chapter 7), led Hayek to rethink his arguments for the market and try to figure out why he wasn't being understood. Before World War II, neither Mises nor Hayek thought there was much difference between their Austrian understanding of economics and that of the emerging neoclassical mainstream. The common belief was that most of what was important about the Austrian tradition had been incorporated into the mainstream economic thought of the time. When Hayek saw economists that he thought of as broadly sharing that understanding beginning to side with Lange (and with Keynes), he must have been not just disappointed but puzzled. How could all of these people who he thought saw economics like he did suddenly take the views they were taking? Much of Hayek's work from the mid-1940s through the early 1950s can be seen as him searching for the answer to this question. We will explore some of this work in Chapter 8.

In his major contribution to the socialist calculation debate, Lange joked that the market socialists should build a statue of Mises in the halls of the planning board to thank him for forcing them to figure out why he was wrong and why planning could work. As it turns out, Lange ended up playing exactly that role for the Austrians by forcing Hayek and others to reconsider and deepen their understanding of how markets worked and to understand why their arguments were so poorly understood by the rest of the economics profession. Lange's work caused Austrians to clarify the uniqueness of their perspective and how it really did differ from that of the mainstream of the discipline. The growth of Austrian economics in the 75 years since the conclusion of the socialist calculation debate owes much to that rethinking process.

7

Austrian Business Cycle Theory and the Hayek-Keynes Debate

While Hayek was debating the socialists, he was also engaged in an equally important debate with the British economist John Maynard Keynes. Hayek and others had built on Mises's early work on business cycles to develop, by the early 1930s, a more complete theory of booms and busts that had become one of the dominant theories in economics.[30] Keynes offered a very different vision of the "macroeconomy," and his explanations of why we had recessions and what to do about them eventually won the day, dominating economics for decades. As with the socialist calculation debate, Hayek was perceived to have lost the debate with Keynes in its immediate aftermath. However, later work has vindicated some of Hayek's criticisms of Keynes, although the verdict of the economics profession on the Austrian theory of the business cycle is not nearly as positive as its view of the Austrian position on economic planning. Austrian economists continue to press the case for their very different understanding of macroeconomics. The Austrian view of macroeconomics is based on the very same elements of the Austrian approach we have emphasized in earlier chapters.

The Austrian theory of the business cycle, which is sometimes known as the Mises-Hayek theory of the business cycle, was first delineated in Mises's 1912 book *The Theory of Money and Credit*. In that book, he drew on a British tradition in monetary theory, which he combined with the theory of capital from his Austrian predecessors and the work of the Swedish economist Knut Wicksell on the role of the interest rate.

The business cycle started with inflation, which Mises understood to mean a supply of money that was in excess of the demand to hold money at the current price level. In *The Theory of Money and Credit*, Mises laid out the cash-balance approach to the demand for money, arguing that the demand for money was a demand to hold balances of real purchasing power. What mattered was what one's money could buy.

If the banking system created more money than the purchasing power people wished to hold, they would spend the excess, driving up prices; this increase in prices was the visible manifestation of the excess supply of money.

Such inflations did not merely cause prices to rise. Mises explained how inflationary expansions in the money supply would lead to an unsustainable economic boom followed by a recession. Specifically, he argued that excess supplies of money, whether created by a central bank or by a poorly designed private banking system, would lead individual banks to lower the *market rate* of interest (i.e., the rate that they charged borrowers) below what Wicksell called the *natural rate* of interest, which was the rate that reflected the actual time preferences of market actors.[31] The challenge for a banking system is that borrowers and lenders cannot directly trade time but instead must trade time in the form of money. A loan represents the movement of wealth through time, from the future to the present for the borrower and from the present to the future for the lender. Austrians see the interest rate as a reflection of those time preferences: how intensely we prefer the present to the future, all other things equal, determines our time preference, and our time preferences then determine the natural interest rate.

The market rate of interest is the result of the interaction between the supply of loanable funds (gathered through private saving) and the demand for such funds (for investment by borrowers). In a well-functioning banking system, the market rate of interest that banks charge is an accurate reflection of those underlying time preferences. In other words, the interest rate that producers pay to borrow funds to begin processes of production is coordinated with the willingness of consumers to sacrifice present consumption in order to obtain greater future consumption.

Mises argued that when inflation is present, banks are able to lend more and will bring in new borrowers by offering them lower interest rates.[32] In modern central banking systems, expansions of the money supply take place when the central bank buys up government-issued bonds either directly from banks or from other bondholders.[33] In either case, the funds the central bank creates to pay for those bonds end up in banks, where they serve as new reserves, most of which can now be lent out to borrowers if the banks offer them a slightly lower interest rate. When those borrowers spend the funds, prices get driven up throughout the economy as a consequence of the credit expansion.

The lower market rate that banks offer also makes it appear as though people's time preferences have changed and that people are saving more and are more willing to wait for future production. The firms that borrow the new funds interpret that signal to mean they can invest more in the early stages of production, lengthening the time until consumable output is produced but getting more of that output as a result. The lower interest rate is taken to mean that longer-term projects are now more profitable, all else equal. However, the public's willingness to wait longer for that greater output has not actually changed. The result is a mismatch between producer expectations and consumer preferences. This intertemporal discoordination is the heart of the Austrian business cycle theory and why the theory sees the boom as unsustainable.

As firms put the newly borrowed funds to work in things like research and development or obtaining raw materials, hiring increases in those industries, driving up wages and the prices of complementary capital goods. This activity is the "boom" part of the business cycle. Mises and Hayek both knew that booms disproportionately affected these sorts of capital goods and knew that any good theory of the business cycle had to explain this phenomenon. The boom goes on as long as the excess supply of money continues, and continues at an increasing rate. Eventually one of two things has to happen: either the inflation stops, leading to the "bust" part of the business cycle, or the inflation continues to ratchet up, leading to what Mises called the "crack-up boom," or the complete collapse of the monetary system due to excessive inflation.[34] In the first scenario, the rise in prices of early-stage factors of production combined with unexpectedly high demand by consumers for consumption goods (resulting from the false interest rate signal) eventually leads producers to realize that their half-completed production processes are no longer profitable. They begin to abandon those projects, laying off workers and idling capital. The boom turns to bust, and the recession begins.

One important note on this theory is that the problems take place during the boom, and the bust is the necessary corrective process. What recessions do is make clear the errors made during the boom (what the Austrians call "malinvestment") and begin the process of reallocating resources to more valued uses. One analogy here is to a hangover from drinking too much alcohol. When you wake up feeling sick the next morning, it's not because you made a bad decision that morning; rather, it's the consequence of the bad decisions you made the night before. Your body feeling sick is its way of repairing the harmful effects of the alcohol. You feel sick, but that feeling is actually evidence that you are getting better as your body eliminates the toxin. One implication of this point for the Austrian understanding of the business cycle is that the right policy during a recession is to let the economy heal itself and that the *last* thing governments should do is to try to generate new inflation to fix the recession. That "fix" would simply recreate the original problem.

As Mises and Hayek developed this theory during the 1920s, it became accepted by a fair number of economists and was one of the major theories in contention to explain booms and busts. While the Austrian theory emphasized the need for interest rate signals generated in the context of a sound banking system with saving leading to capital accumulation and the expansion of output, the most widely accepted competing theories focused on consumption and spending as the keys to economic health. In his 1930 book *A Treatise on Money*, Keynes systematized some of those ideas, also linking them to Wicksell's work in ways that partially overlapped with the Austrian theory.[35] Hayek reviewed the book in a lengthy two-part essay in *Economica*, one of the major economics journals.[36] His review was critical, although also sympathetic in certain ways, and focused on the way in which Keynes's use of aggregates to model key relationships among saving, investment, employment, and output obscured important issues. In particular, Hayek argued that Keynes's book overlooked the microeconomic adjustment processes that were at the heart of a sound understanding of economic fluctuations and that characterized the Austrian theory. That point was especially relevant in the context of understanding the role of capital and the adjustments among the stages of production that Mises and Hayek had described. Keynes's book glossed over the relationships among relative prices in his quest to develop an aggregative "macroeconomics."

In the years between the publication of Keynes's *A Treatise on Money* and his 1936 book *The General Theory of Employment, Interest, and Money*, Hayek and a number of his students continued to press the case that the Austrian theory was superior to the ideas Keynes was working on.[37] One of the problems the Austrians faced was that, as the Great Depression that had begun in 1929 worsened and spread globally, the Austrian prescription of letting markets heal themselves grew less and less politically tenable. Previous busts, even the fairly severe one in the 1890s, had never been this deep—as unemployment in the United States in early 1933 was almost 25 percent—and had never lasted this long—as the depression extended into the mid-1930s. Lacking a positive program of policy reform, the Austrians were vulnerable as the inevitable cries for government to "do something" arose in countries around the world.

In the meantime, Keynes faced two options in the face of Hayek's extended criticisms of his 1930 book: he could take those criticisms into account and revise his thinking in a way that incorporated them, or he could push forward in the same direction that Hayek saw as mistaken. Keynes chose the latter: *The General Theory* removed the Wicksellian elements of the *Treatise on Money* and expanded the use of aggregates disconnected from any true microeconomic foundations. In its simplest formulation, Keynes argued that total expenditures (Y) for a closed economy could be understood as the sum of consumption spending (C), investment spending (I), and government spending (G): $Y = C + I + G$. The volume of expenditures was subsequently linked to the volume of employment, and declines in spending could get an economy stuck in an "unemployment equilibrium." Keynes saw consumption as a fairly stable variable but argued that investment was much less stable and that it depended on what he called the "animal spirits," or the expectations of entrepreneurs. If entrepreneurial expectations turned negative, causing I to drop, there was no built-in mechanism by which a market economy would offset that decline in spending with other forms of spending. The key to that claim, in Keynes's system, was his belief that there was no necessary connection between investment and savings. Investment depended on the animal spirits, while savings depended on total household income.[38]

This was in dramatic contrast to the Austrian view—which was also held by the Swedes (such as Wicksell) and the British monetary theorists—that investment and savings were connected by the interest rate. In their "loanable funds" approach to the interest rate, market rates of interest, as noted earlier, coordinated the time preferences of lenders and borrowers. If the Austrians were right, a decline in entrepreneurial expectations would decrease the demand to borrow. The drop in demand would lower interest rates, and the lower interest rates would discourage saving and thereby encourage consumption. Similarly, if households decided to save more, the Keynesians would see that change as causing a decline in consumption spending that could not be offset, but the Austrians argued that a higher supply of loanable funds would cause the interest rate to fall, which would make it cheaper to borrow, increasing investment spending to both match the increased saving and offset the fall in consumption. In the Austrian theory, the interest rate coordinated investment and saving. In Keynes's theory, no such coordination was possible, leaving economies vulnerable to the whims of entrepreneurial expectations.[39]

The policy implications of each view are straightforward. In the simple Keynesian model, the decline in investment spending will not be offset by rising consumption spending, but *can* be offset by an increase in government spending. Thus, the Keynesians argued that to avoid recessions, governments must compensate for changes in private spending by unbalancing their budgets. As recessions appeared, governments should spend more and tax less, using that deficit to "prime the pump" of the private sector and restore full-employment equilibrium. They also argued that in times of high growth, governments should run surpluses to fund the deficits needed in the bad times. It's worth noting that such thinking has led to decades of nearly constant deficits. Politicians have no incentive to run the surpluses required to fund deficits because it would mean taxing their constituents more and spending less on them. That said, the Keynesian vision was one where elected officials, with help from economists, could steer the economy between the Scylla of inflationary overheating and the Charybdis of recession. Economies, they argued, were not self-correcting.

By contrast, the Austrian view was that markets were self-correcting *as long as they had a properly functioning banking system* and as long as other poor policy choices were not hampering market processes. For the Austrians, it was possible for markets to be self-correcting under the right set of institutions and policies, whereas the Keynesian vision denied that such self-correction was even possible. In the Keynesian view, it was only by sheer luck that an economy would end up at full employment without government intervention.[40]

The core disagreement between these contrasting visions, I would argue, is in how Hayek and Keynes understood the role of capital and the related issue of economic calculation.[41] Keynesian aggregation meant that the I in $C + I + G = Y$ became a proxy for all the investment spending in the economy. At that level of aggregation, the Austrian view that there is a structure of capital extending from the early stages of research and development through the later stages near consumption, and that the key to economic growth is allocating resources across this structure in a sustainable way, is not part of the picture. For the Austrians, the role of economic calculation is to enable entrepreneurs to make use of prices, *including the interest rate*, to determine how resources should be used across space and through time.

The interest rate can, from this perspective, be understood as the differences in prices among the various stages of production. When the interest rate changed, the Austrians understood that this would signal entrepreneurs to adjust their spending across the structure of production. Higher interest rates would shorten production processes and encourage relatively more spending closer to consumption. Lower rates would lengthen production processes and encourage investment in the earlier stages of production. In other words, by disaggregating the I of investment into multiple stages coordinated by the interest rate, the Austrians' conception of capital enabled them to explain the self-correcting features of the market. Translated into Keynesian terms, changes in I would be offset by opposite movements in C, obviating the need for an increase in G to prevent a recession. Without the Wicksellian focus on interest rates and without a theory of capital, of course there was no way for Keynes to theorize a self-correcting process to offset declines in investment spending.

The debate between Hayek and Keynes in the 1930s, like the socialist calculation debate taking place contemporaneously, was really about the nature of a complex capital-using economy and the role of prices in enabling entrepreneurs to best allocate resources using monetary calculation. One way of understanding the Austrian theory of the business cycle is that it is a story of prices sending out false signals due to government mismanagement. As central banks inflated, they pushed market rates of interest below natural rates, sending out a wrong signal about household time preferences, leading entrepreneurs to make systematic errors by overestimating how much consumption spending would take place in the future. Their attempts to plan for that future consumption are the boom, and the eventual correction of their errors is the bust. Just as Mises and Hayek had argued that market prices are necessary for rational resource allocation in general, so they argued in their business cycle theory that a market-driven interest rate is necessary for rational resource allocation through time. And like in the calculation debate, the Austrian policy conclusion in the debate with Keynes was that, under the right institutions (e.g., private property and limits on government intervention), market prices would do the job better than the alternatives.

The question, then, is why we had the Great Depression and why we continue to have the booms and busts of the business cycle if markets are supposedly self-correcting. The answer is that the self-correction processes will only work effectively if the rules of the game are right. In the case of the Great Depression, Austrians have argued that the world of the 1920s (as well as the 1930s and 1940s) lacked the right rules. During the 1920s, the Federal Reserve System created an excessive supply of money, which fueled an Austrian-style artificial boom (much like it did in the housing boom of the mid-2000s). Once the crash happened in 1929, the federal government embarked on a number of policies that prevented the bust from quickly correcting the errors of the boom, as it had in previous recessions. The Fed didn't just stop inflating; it actually decreased the money supply by more than 30 percent between 1930 and 1933. Had prices and wages been able to fall fairly rapidly in tandem, the recession might not have been too severe. But the Hoover administration persuaded industry to keep wages high as prices fell, and the protectionism of the Smoot-Hawley tariff also enabled some industries to maintain higher wages. The combination of falling prices and more slowly falling wages raised the real cost of labor, leading to the high unemployment rates that characterized the Great Depression. The various policies of the New Deal under Roosevelt continued to prevent market prices from properly adjusting and created a great deal of uncertainty about the future of the market economy, which made the recovery of private investment particularly slow.

The Great Depression is evidence not of the inherent instability of capitalism, nor of the market economy's inability to self-correct, but rather illustrates how bad institutions and poor policy choices can both disrupt market coordination and prevent markets from self-correcting. In doing so, those institutions and policies can set into motion artificial booms that lead to long and deep busts with tremendous human costs. Properly interpreted, the Great Depression largely vindicates the Austrian approach.[42]

Unfortunately, the judgment of the economics profession, as well as of the political class, was that Keynes won this debate.

The Keynesian model quickly took over, more or less creating modern "macroeconomics." By the 1940s, the Austrian approach had been decisively rejected, with only a very small group still believing it had explanatory power. To some degree, that rejection was because the Austrians could not put forth a positive vision of reform and recovery in the depths of the Depression, while the Keynesians, however wrong they might have been, could. In addition, Hayek decided not to write a review of *The General Theory*. He offered multiple reasons why over the years, and it's not clear whether such a review could have overcome both the desire to "do something" and the ways in which Keynesianism flattered the pretensions of politicians by giving them an illusion of control and a rationalization for abandoning the long-held wisdom of balanced budgets. Hayek's 1941 book *The Pure Theory of Capital* was an attempt to restate the issues, and it did include a brief critique of Keynes's book toward the end, but Hayek's book was too dense and too late to capture the attention of economists or policymakers.[43] A reenvisioning of the Austrian theory that could talk in a meaningful way about institutional reform would have to wait until the failures of the broadly Keynesian model in the 1960s and 1970s opened up the opportunity.

Hayek on Prices, Knowledge, and the Nature of Economics

As Hayek engaged in both the socialist calculation debate and the debate with Keynes, he struggled to understand how his fellow economists had come to such a different view of both how markets work and the very nature of economics as a discipline.[44] For both Mises and Hayek, any proper approach to economics had to start with the perceptions and beliefs of the actors, which meant that economics could not create models that made strong assumptions about what those actors know. Their approach also put the focus of economics on understanding how markets and other institutions enable people to learn from each other despite the fact that knowledge is contextual, hard to articulate, and dispersed.

As noted at the end of Chapter 6, one way of seeing Hayek's work from the mid-1930s until the early 1950s is as an attempt to figure out why he was perceived as having lost both of those debates. This process led to him rethinking the role that knowledge played in the market economy and in how economists talked about the market. More specifically, he began to reconceptualize the function of prices, and he was forced to more clearly articulate just what the task of economics was. During the period in which Hayek participated in those two debates, economics was undergoing some fundamental changes. Those changes made it harder for Hayek to communicate the essential Austrian insights he derived from Menger, Mises, and others. With a new audience of economists who were trained to see the discipline in a different way, Hayek had to offer a different formulation of the Austrian perspective that would, he hoped, be more rhetorically effective given the changes in how economics was done.

Early on, Hayek pinpointed the problem as being with the centrality that the concept of equilibrium had taken on in economics. Whereas the Austrians had, from Menger on, focused on the market *process* and the dynamic properties of the market, the economics profession in the 1920s and 1930s had narrowed down the task of economics to describing the properties of economic equilibria. Rather than explain the ways in which economies responded to change, the goal was to see whether particular equilibrium outcomes—especially ones with optimality properties—were possible and stable, and to see how exogenous change would lead to a new equilibrium. These exercises in "comparative statics" contrasted with the process-oriented dynamism of the Austrian approach.

In 1937, Hayek tried to clarify the conditions necessary for economic equilibrium to hold and what those conditions implied for economic analysis. In his paper "Economics and Knowledge," Hayek proceeded to define equilibrium in terms of the knowledge of economic actors. He argued that what it means for an economy to be in equilibrium is that

> the foresight of the different members of the society is in a special sense correct. It must be correct in the sense that every person's plan is based on the expectation of just those actions of other people which those other people intend to perform and that all these plans are based on the expectation of the same set of external facts, so that under certain conditions nobody will have any reason to change his plans.[45]

Put differently, that correct foresight is not a "precondition" for equilibrium but rather "the defining characteristic

of a state of equilibrium." With this understanding of equilibrium, Hayek put knowledge front and center in understanding the task of economics. If equilibrium was to be the
centerpiece of the discipline, then economists would have to
get serious about talking about knowledge. And if equilibrium was defined as "correct foresight," and if it was to be
useful for explaining the real world, the fundamental question became how it was possible for human beings to come to
possess correct expectations of the external facts and of each
other's plans. Suddenly, economics becomes all about how
knowledge is acquired and used.

Later in that essay, Hayek said that the claim that markets
tend toward equilibrium must be understood as saying

> that, under certain conditions, the knowledge and
> intentions of the different members of society are
> supposed to come more and more into agreement or,
> to put the same thing in less general and less exact
> but more concrete terms, that the expectations of
> the people and particularly of the entrepreneurs will
> become more and more correct.[46]

This claim implies that in examining the effectiveness
of markets, or of any other set of economic institutions, we
should be exploring how well they enable people to learn from

each other. If markets empirically tend toward equilibrium, it must be because something about markets makes it possible for people to learn about what other people want and how intensely they value things so that people's expectations can become increasingly correct. The questions, therefore, are whether that happens, how it happens, and what sorts of institutions are best at making it happen.

Hayek's definitive statement about the answers to those questions came a few years later, in 1945. In what is perhaps his most well-known article and one of the most cited articles in the history of economics, Hayek argued in "The Use of Knowledge in Society" that what made it possible for people to learn from each other in the marketplace was the price system.[47] Prices serve as surrogates for the underlying knowledge possessed by market actors and thereby enable people to better coordinate their expectations and actions with each other. Hayek framed the problem of social order as a matter of overcoming a division of knowledge that is parallel to the division of labor that has always been central to understanding the market. He also argued that the key question is what sort of economic system, or, more specifically, whether the decentralized planning and competition of the market or the centralized planning of socialism, will make "fuller use . . . of the existing knowledge."[48] He goes on to make clear that the knowledge in question is not just the sort that can be put into words or numbers but also the knowledge of "the particular circumstances of time and place," which "cannot be conveyed to any central authority in statistical form."[49]

The price system enables us to communicate this information through the way prices change as actors decide to buy or sell, or to not buy or not sell. More precisely, prices serve as knowledge "surrogates." They do not actually communicate information, but they enable us to act *as if we had that information*—the inarticulate knowledge of the billions of people participating in global markets. No one knows everything, but the price system enables our fields of vision to overlap such that we can make knowledge available for others to use. Hayek also reminds us, in that article, that for prices to perform this function to the best of their ability, they cannot be too rigid. Price ceilings or floors, for example, weaken the accuracy of the signal being sent by prices because they prevent prices from reacting to changes in knowledge on either side of the market. Similarly, when prices are too mercurial, as a result of distortions from misguided policy, they are like radio signals masked by static. Actors do not know which changes are real and which are artifices of policy. Inflation is perhaps the best example of a policy that increases the difficulty of determining what a particular price change means, thereby making it harder for entrepreneurs and consumers to coordinate their expectations. And consider our discussion of Austrian business cycle theory in Chapter 7: the way inflation drives the market rate of interest below the natural rate is a perfect example of prices providing a noisy signal as a result of misguided policy. The errors that constitute the boom of the cycle are consequences of prices not being free to tell the truth.

Hayek's argument that prices serve as knowledge surrogates can be seen as the obverse of Mises's work on monetary calculation that we discussed in Chapter 5.[50] Whereas Hayek focused on the role prices play interpersonally in making knowledge usable by more people, Mises's work on monetary calculation stressed the role prices play for individual choosers as they attempt to navigate an uncertain world. Put another way, Mises's work looked at the "of human action" part of the definition of spontaneous order, and Hayek's looked at the "but not human design" part. In terms that Austrians sometimes use, Mises was taking a praxeological approach by showing how prices helped individual rational action, whereas Hayek was looking at the catallaxy (or unintended order created by exchange) that prices enabled to emerge.

The key point is that these two ways of looking at prices and knowledge are all part of one process. Hayek's papers on knowledge in this period did not say much about entre-preneurship or monetary calculation or the role of profit and loss. In turn, Mises's work on monetary calculation in both the socialist calculation debate and then later in *Human Action* did not say a lot about these Hayekian arguments (although they were noted). Each had their rhetorical focus, largely driven by the audiences they were addressing in different contexts. But together they offer a seamless understanding of the way prices guide the behavior of individual actors by making our (often private) knowledge accessible to others through the prices and profit/loss signals of the marketplace. Prices inform our actions before the fact, and profits and losses (which are the conse-quences of a new set of prices emerging) tell us whether our decisions created value. Those profit and loss figures, and the new set of prices that produced them, inform the next round of decisions. Putting Mises and Hayek together in this way pro-vides the core of the Austrian understanding of the microeco-nomic process, and it helps us understand why various forms of socialism, and government planning in general, can never replace or outperform the ability of market prices to make use of the dispersed, contextual, and tacit knowledge that perme-ates economic decisionmaking. Market prices help us overcome the "knowledge problem" in a way nothing else can. They are necessary, although not sufficient, for economic progress.

As Hayek was rethinking the guts of economics, he was also rethinking its place in the structure of knowledge. He thought that the socialists and the Keynesians had misunderstood how markets work, but he also came to believe that they had done so because they had also misunderstood the nature and task of economics as a social science. In the late 1940s, Hayek tried to make the case for the subjectivism of economics in a series of essays that became his 1952 book *The Counter-Revolution of Science.*[51] The essence of his argument was that a science of human action could not treat humans the same way that the natural sciences treated the objects of the physical world. Humans acted purposively on the basis of their perceptions of reality. One could not really *understand* human behavior if one only charted the physical movements of humans. One had to understand what objects *mean* to humans to understand their choices, and doing so required that one begin any social science with the perceptions of the actors.

Economics, like all other social sciences, had to begin from the inside and work outward. How humans perceived the world and how those perceptions led to their actions was at the core of economics: "So far as human actions are concerned the things are what the acting people think they are."[52] What makes an object a tool, or money, or valuable in general, is not physical properties of the object but the purposes to which humans believe they can put that object. The "data" from which economic theorizing begins, then, are the ideas, thoughts, and perceptions that actors have. Those "data" are not given to anyone in their entirety, and the task of economics is to explain how actions based on subjective perceptions produce patterns of orderly, but unintended, consequences in the social world. Hayek offers a strong defense of long-standing Austrian subjectivism, pointing explicitly to Mises's work as the exemplar of this approach. The failure of the economics of Hayek's time—and arguably also of the economics of today—was that it wrongly attempted to apply the methods of the natural sciences, which are appropriate for objects of study that neither perceive nor choose, to the social sciences, where perception, meaning, and intention are essential to the objects of study.

Rather than solving for deterministic equilibria, Hayek argued for what he called the "compositive" method in economics and the social sciences.[53] By "compositive," Hayek meant that we should start with the simple phenomena of individual choice and build from them an explanation of the complex phenomena of society. Economics was not about "explaining" individual choices, as that was the task of psychology. Rather, it was about explaining how orderly patterns of outcomes would emerge, unplanned, from individual choices. As we noted earlier, in *Human Action*, Mises points to Menger's theory of the origin of money as the archetype of what Hayek is calling the compositive approach to economics. What both Mises and Hayek were doing was showing how a subjectivist approach to economics could still generate objective knowledge about the laws by which social interaction proceeded, and about the consequences of ignoring them.

Understanding economics as a coordination problem means that the task of the discipline is to explain how people with subjective and partial knowledge nonetheless manage to coordinate their knowledge and expectations with anonymous others through the institutions of the market, especially prices. The compositive method enables Austrians to focus on the process by which that (often less-than-full) coordination takes place, rather than describing in detail the features of full and complete coordination in equilibrium. By wrongly thinking that describing beautiful equilibria through the more prestigious methods of the natural sciences could explain how real markets operate, and by erroneously believing that identifying the conditions that produced equilibrium was the appropriate method of economics—rather than showing how order emerges spontaneously under the right rules and institutions—economists got off on a wrong track that rendered them susceptible to the errors of both socialism and Keynesianism. Hayek's work on knowledge, prices, and subjectivism was central to the rebirth of Austrian economics in the decades to follow.

9

Competition, Entrepreneurship, and the Discovery Process of the Market

Hayek's work in the 1940s and 1950s, along with Mises's *Human Action*, was largely ignored by the mainstream of the profession. The general equilibrium paradigm had taken over microeconomics, and Keynesianism quickly dominated macroeconomics. The Austrians of the interwar period were either dying off or abandoning that paradigm for one part or another of the mainstream.[54] Until around 1960, the Austrian tradition was being kept alive only by Mises at New York

University, Hayek at the Committee on Social Thought at the University of Chicago, and Ludwig Lachmann at the University of Witwatersrand in South Africa, with the help of the Foundation for Economic Education in New York City. However, by the early 1960s, the green shoots of what eventually would become the Austrian revival were visible, as Mises's PhD student Israel Kirzner secured a position at NYU and began his decades of contributions to Austrian economics. In addition, Murray Rothbard, also in New York City at the time, had joined Mises's seminar at NYU while finishing his PhD at Columbia University. Rothbard's contributions in the 1960s would also be an important part of the Austrian revival. In this chapter, I look at how Kirzner's work reinvigorated Austrian market process theory, and in the next chapter, I look at the revival of Austrian macroeconomics, much of which was a continuation of, and critical response to, some of Rothbard's work in the 1960s.

By the 1960s, mainstream microeconomics was dominated by general equilibrium theory—in particular, the model of perfect competition. This approach had already started to become part of the theoretical consensus between the world wars, prompting Hayek to write "The Meaning of Competition" in 1946.[55] In the 1960s and early 1970s, that theoretical consensus affected policymaking, including the way in which the courts and agencies like the Federal Trade Commission thought about issues of competition, monopoly, and antitrust. The model of perfect competition described the conditions necessary for optimal resource allocation. Specifically, it argued that if there were a large number of small firms, each of which produced an identical product and took market prices as given; if those firms had freedom of entry and exit from the market; and if market actors had perfect, relevant knowledge, the market would allocate all goods to their highest-valued uses and produce the maximum value possible. Neither firms nor households could do anything different that made them better off without making someone else worse off. If the conditions of perfect competition held across all markets, the economy would be in general equilibrium. Given the optimality properties of perfect competition, it was a short step for policymakers to try to make the real world look like the model. The result was, for example, a number of merger cases where even small firms were prohibited from merging on the grounds that it would reduce the number of firms and increase their size, thereby reducing the "competitiveness" of the market.

In his 1946 lecture, Hayek pointed out the essence of the problem with the perfect competition model: it mistook the idea of competition as a static state of affairs for the more correct understanding of competition as a dynamic process. That process, he argued, was one through which knowledge was spread. The key assumption in the perfect competition model was that actors had perfect knowledge. Hayek, as he had done in the socialist calculation debate and the debate with Keynes, noted that such an assumption assumed away the key problem: "it is only through the process of competition that the facts will be discovered."[56] He later added: "The function of competition is here precisely to teach us *who* will serve us well."[57] By creating a model in which people are assumed to know everything they need to know, mainstream economics had obliterated what the Austrians saw as the key function of competitive markets. Markets enable us, as we discussed in the previous chapter, to overcome the limits of our partial and inarticulate knowledge and to learn from others in order to better coordinate with them. Descriptions of a hypothetical perfectly coordinated market might have a certain aesthetic appeal, but they do little to explain how markets enable us to achieve the degree of coordination we are capable of, imperfect as it may be.

Kirzner entered this discussion in full force with his 1973 book *Competition and Entrepreneurship*.[58] Kirzner's book was a methodical walk through the various models of competition and monopoly used by economists of the time, critically assessing them in light of the Austrian emphasis on process and learning as opposed to equilibrium. What Kirzner saw as missing from those models was the entrepreneur. Kirzner's contribution in the book was to offer a Misesian solution (the entrepreneur) to a Hayekian problem (how do competitive markets help us learn?), and then to use that understanding of the market to illustrate the weaknesses in the various equilibrium-bound models of the mainstream. In laying out a vision of the entrepreneurial market process and explicitly placing it in the context of both the questions and the scholarship of mainstream economics, Kirzner's book was the work most significantly responsible for the revival of Austrian economics that began in the late 1970s and has continued to strengthen over the succeeding 40 years.

The entrepreneur, in Kirzner's work, is the person who sees opportunities to remove the mutual ignorance of market actors. To return to our earlier example, imagine apples selling for $2 on one side of the street and $3 on the other. Sellers of $2 apples are ignorant of their ability to perhaps fetch a higher price, and buyers of $3 apples are ignorant of cheaper apples across the street. Entrepreneurship, for Kirzner, is the act of being *alert* to such opportunities. In their ignorance, parties on both sides of the street might well be maximizing utility and profits *given their perception of their opportunities.*

Within their perceived means-ends framework, they are doing the best they can. And until the moment of recognition, the entrepreneur too is operating under the same means-ends framework. However, when the entrepreneur recognizes their mutual ignorance and sees an opportunity to profit by, say, buying apples on one side of the street for $2.25 and selling them on the other for $2.75, she now has an entirely new perception of the relevant means and ends. And when she acts on that new perception, the apple-market actors on both sides of the street see that their perceptions were erroneous as well. All parties were utterly ignorant of an opportunity to be better off, and for actions to be better coordinated, until the entrepreneur was alert to it.

These acts of entrepreneurship are, for Kirzner, the essence of competition. When our entrepreneur outbids other buyers by offering $2.25 for apples, she is engaging in competitive behavior, just as she is when she undersells the $3 apples by offering them for $2.75. In Kirzner's view, competition *is* entrepreneurial, and entrepreneurship *is* competitive. What competition and entrepreneurship do, in the view of Austrian economists, is peel back the "sheer ignorance" of market actors. This sheer ignorance is distinguished from other forms of ignorance by the fact that we do not know what it is we do not know. Kirzner distinguishes between "search" and "discovery."[59] When we search for something, we know what it is we're looking for, and we begin a methodical process of finding it. Searches are subject to maximization considerations: at some point, the costs of searching might be high enough to make further search unwarranted. When we search, we are taking a particular means-ends framework as given and are trying to maximize. For example, "How do I find out the address of my friend in Cleveland?"

Search behavior *is* part of the market, of course, but it is not the same thing as discovery, which involves the removal of sheer ignorance. Suppose, while finding that friend's address, I discover that another friend has moved to Cleveland unbeknownst to me. I could not have searched for that friend's new address, because I did not know that I did not know it. This act of discovery, which involves realizing that I was not aware of my own ignorance, is what characterizes entrepreneurship. Our apple sellers did not know that they did not correctly perceive the opportunities in front of them. When the entrepreneur perceives them, she has made a discovery, and her subsequent action will make others in the market aware of the new opportunities as well. This is the learning process that Hayek identified in "Economics and Knowledge" in 1937, and it is the entrepreneur, so central to Mises's work, especially in *Human Action*, whose alertness ignites the new learning and makes the resulting knowledge available to others. In words Hayek used in a later essay, competition is a "discovery procedure."[60] Entrepreneurial action is how we overcome our mutual ignorance, and it constitutes the process by which prices move to better serve as surrogates for our ever-changing knowledge.

Kirzner's focus was on a very precise point in economic theory: explaining how it was possible that economies might move from situations of sheer ignorance to ones with greater degrees of coordination. In this way, he was attempting to explain the operation of the invisible hand, or, in the language of his contemporaries, how it was possible for an economy to tend toward equilibrium. We can also reconcile Kirzner's view with our earlier discussion of capital and calculation. Once entrepreneurs perceive an opportunity, they must then marshal the resources to take advantage of it, which entails pulling together complementary capital goods (including "human capital") and formulating a plan of action and a budget on the basis of existing market prices. That entrepreneurial plan is put to the market test, with the resulting profits or losses informing entrepreneurs of the accuracy of their perceptions. They then engage in another round of opportunity perception, planning, and budgeting and repeat the process. This is the dynamic of the market process, driven by entrepreneurial perceptions of both what consumers want and how best to produce it. Entrepreneurs are like scientists, proposing a hypothesis in the form of a budget and production plan and then testing it in a world of uncertainty against the wants of consumers, with profit and loss being the guide to success.

This vision of competition and entrepreneurship is very different from the mainstream's models of perfect competition and of industrial organization more generally. The various models employed by mainstream economists attempt to show the social welfare implications of different types of market structures. As noted, perfect competition delivers optimality, and any deviation from that model will reduce the total gains to producers and consumers. Monopoly power is defined by mainstream economics as the failure of any of the assumptions of perfect competition to hold, especially the assumptions about the size of firms, their influence over prices, and the homogeneity of their products. Larger firms, firms that have influence over prices, or firms that differentiate their products all disrupt the "perfection" of perfect competition. The result of this approach has not only been that all real-world deviations from perfect competition are seen as "market failures," but also that economists think they can know what the ideal structure of an industry "should" be. This view informs federal regulation and antitrust legislation to this day.[61]

The problem from an Austrian perspective is that these models suffer from a pretense of knowledge. There is no way for anyone to know what the "right" structure for an industry is. We cannot know ahead of time how many firms should be competing or how big or small they should be. Figuring that out is exactly what the competitive entrepreneurial market process does. When firms merge, for example, they are testing out an entrepreneurial hypothesis that a larger firm will be better able to create value and profit than will two small ones. The only test of that hypothesis is the profit-and-loss test of a genuine market. Neither economists, nor judges, nor bureaucrats possess the knowledge necessary to know the ideal market structure, and there's no reason to believe that deviations from the perfectly competitive outcome are, in any sense of the term, "failures." Firms make use of all kinds of competitive strategies to profit by better serving consumers.

Austrian economists, in contrast, are much more interested in what sort of institutional framework best enables the process of entrepreneurial discovery to serve consumers. Austrians do not pretend to know which market structure will do so; rather, they want to make it possible for entrepreneurs to figure out that structure through rivalrous competition. In a competitive market, prices and other signals will provide entrepreneurs with the incentives and knowledge necessary to more correctly anticipate what consumers want and to discover whether their views of the future are right.

Note the implications for our understanding of monopoly. Rather than seeing evidence of monopoly in deviations from the perfectly competitive ideal, such as a firm's power over price, large size, or differentiated products, Austrians see all of these as ways in which firms engage in competition. Mergers, as noted above, are a competitive maneuver, but so are the various ways in which firms tinker with their products to make them different from similar ones produced by other firms. Adding a camera to a cellphone was not monopolistic behavior—it was a form of competition, offering a potentially more valuable product to consumers. Cars with backup cameras are another example of competition by differentiation. These are all attempts to discover, in the face of ignorance and uncertainty, what goods consumers value, and how best to make those goods, through competitive entrepreneurial behavior.

True monopoly, by contrast, is when actual or potential entrepreneurs are prevented from exercising their entrepreneurial judgment by legal barriers. The most obvious examples of this phenomenon are when firms are required to have government licenses to provide specific goods and services—as are the taxicab companies in many cities—making it impossible for entrepreneurs—such as Uber or Lyft drivers—to compete with them. Legal barriers to entry (and exit) choke off the discovery process of the market by preventing entrepreneurs who perceive new opportunities, either for a closely competing product or for a way to provide a slightly differentiated version of a current product, from putting their perceptions into action. Firms with protection from such competition will indeed, as the perfect competition model predicts, produce less and/or lower-quality output while having room to charge higher prices. But real monopoly power is about protection from the new ideas of others. Real competition might be called "permissionless innovation," in the sense that competitive markets serve as testing grounds for rivalrous conceptions of how to best serve consumers.[62] For Austrians, competition policy is about allowing the discovery process of the market to work unhindered by legally-imposed barriers to entry or other protections for incumbents, calls for which often come from the incumbents themselves. Freedom of entry and a level playing field for all competitors will ensure that entrepreneurial profit-seeking generates economic coordination and the most value for consumers.

10

Modern Austrian Monetary Theory and Macroeconomics

In the same way that Kirzner's work in the 1960s and early 1970s laid the microeconomic foundations for the Austrian revival, Murray Rothbard's work, particularly his 1963 book *America's Great Depression*, was the inspiration for much of the revival's research in macroeconomics.[63] Rothbard's book offered an updated version of the Austrian theory of the business cycle in its opening section, followed by a discussion of the monetary expansion of the 1920s that led to the crash in 1929, and it concluded with several chapters on the Hoover years and the ways in which Hoover's policies exacerbated the effects of the crash. Notably, the first chapter's elaboration of the cycle theory included a criticism of fractional reserve banking and a defense of a 100 percent reserve gold-based system as the only protection against inflation and business cycles. That argument was controversial among younger Austrians at the time, and their various attempts to offer alternative frameworks for monetary theory and policy were central in igniting several advances in Austrian macroeconomics in the revival period.

One point to clarify off the top is that "Austrian macroeconomics" is not a contradiction in terms. For many years, Austrians, including Mises and Hayek, were scornful of the whole idea of "macroeconomics," and many Austrians still are. Their main objection is that economics is of necessity all about relative prices and microeconomic coordination. The idea that aggregate variables—such as consumption, investment, and government spending in the Keynesian model—had causal efficacy and could be understood in some way separate from microeconomic choices was rejected, as we saw in Hayek's criticisms of Keynes. Those criticisms are reasonable, and perhaps modern Austrian macroeconomics would be better termed modern Austrian *monetary economics*, but there is still value in the term "macroeconomics." The Austrian approach tries to answer many of the same central questions as modern macroeconomics, but it does so with a significantly different approach. Once we realize that disturbances to the supply of money will have systematic distorting effects across the entire set of relative money prices, "macroeconomics" can be understood as the attempt to understand the causes and consequences of those systematic, economy-wide patterns of price distortions and microeconomic discoordination. Paraphrasing the Austrian economist Roger Garrison, there might be macroeconomic questions, but there are only microeconomic answers. Understanding why economies are subject to aggregate fluctuations such as recessions and inflation requires that we look for a systematic culprit for those economy-wide "macroeconomic" problems. The explanations will be found in the way that monetary mischief distorts the microeconomic price-coordination process. This is the legitimate domain of an *Austrian* macroeconomics.

The three major extensions of Austrian monetary theory and macroeconomics during the revival era are the development of the theory and history of free banking in the work of Lawrence White and George Selgin, the use of monetary equilibrium theory as the basis for monetary economics and macroeconomics in both Selgin's book and my own work, and Roger Garrison's various extensions of Austrian business cycle theory, particularly his book *Time and Money*.[64] All of that work has subsequently been applied to a variety of issues, but particularly to understanding the causes and consequences of the financial crisis and Great Recession of the 2000s.

The first challenge to the Rothbardian framework in Austrian macroeconomics came in 1984 with the publication of Lawrence White's *Free Banking in Britain*. White offered a brief theoretical model that described how competitive, fractional reserve banks (what he termed a "free banking" system) would avoid inflation and therefore business cycles. He used that framework to explore the history of the Scottish banking system in the first half of the 19th century. White argued that the mostly competitive fractional reserve system of that era was quite effective at keeping inflation in check and was subject to very few bank runs with very little in the way of losses to depositors. He also offered a revised categorization of the monetary thinkers of the time, enabling him to identify a "Free Banking School" distinct from either side of the long-standing Currency School versus Banking School debate. White's combination of theory and history offered an alternative theoretical framework for Austrian monetary theory as well as an alternative set of monetary institutions for preventing inflation and the business cycle.

Four years later, George Selgin expanded White's treatment of the theoretical argument for why competitive, fractional-reserve banking could ensure that the supply of money was linked to the demand to hold money. Maintaining that relationship would ensure that the market rate of interest was linked to the natural rate of interest, thereby avoiding any booms and, therefore, any busts. Underlying that argument is the idea that money is half of every exchange and that excesses or deficiencies in the supply of money will "spill over" into real goods and services. As discussed in Chapter 7, people's demand for money is a demand to hold real balances, or a particular amount of purchasing power. We demand money (when we hold it) because it provides us the service of being available for use whenever we might need it, which is crucial in a world of uncertainty. Another key observation is that money arrives in our balances in routine ways, such as when we are paid for work or sell an asset. This makes it possible for our actual holdings of money at any point in time to differ from our desired holdings. When our actual holdings of money equal our desired holdings, there is no impetus to either spend excess balances or restrict our consumption to let those balances build up. This situation is known as monetary equilibrium. However, when we find ourselves persistently holding more purchasing power than we wish, we will engage in a portfolio swap by purchasing goods and services, reducing our holdings of money and increasing our holdings of those other things. Conversely, if we find ourselves persistently short on real purchasing power, we will do the one thing totally within our control to remedy the situation, which is to restrict our consumption to allow our money balances to build back up to where we want them.

When we spend excess money balances or reduce our consumption to rebuild our money holdings, prices will rise and fall, respectively (all else being equal). These changes are monetary inflation and deflation as seen from a monetary equilibrium perspective. Inflation is an excess supply of money, and deflation is a deficient supply.[65] Both can be avoided if the monetary system is able to produce the quantity of money that matches the demand for real money balances. Selgin's argument was that a free banking system in which the money created by banks was backed fractionally by some commodity was capable of maintaining monetary equilibrium and avoiding both inflation and deflation.

Under a free banking system, the demand for money in the form of bank-issued liabilities, such as checking accounts or currency, represents savings, in that when we allow our holdings of those liabilities to rise, we are providing loanable funds to the banking system. The supply of bank-issued money is connected with the demand for loanable funds, or investment. When banks issue loans based on the savings/deposits of the holders of their checking account dollars, they are providing investment funds to entrepreneurs. Roughly speaking, when a banking system maintains monetary equilibrium by producing the quantity of money that people wish to hold, it is also keeping investment equal to saving.[66] That equality is crucial, because it implies that the market rate of interest is an accurate reflection of the underlying natural rate. If so, then maintaining monetary equilibrium will avoid inflation, deflation, and the business cycle.

In that book, and then in a later monograph, Selgin elaborated on how the price level can be affected by both monetary and real factors.[67] The discussion above showed how price inflation and deflation can result from disequilibria in the money market. However, these are not the only factors that can affect the overall price level. Changes in productivity can do so as well. As economies get more productive, the prices of goods and services should fall. What we would expect to see in a healthy economy where monetary equilibrium is being roughly maintained is a falling price level. The point is that, from an Austrian perspective, one cannot simply look at the price level and know if there is problematic inflation or deflation. Price inflation or deflation that comes from monetary disequilibrium will do damage, but price changes that come from productivity changes are desirable, because those price movements reflect changes in underlying scarcities in precisely the way Hayek and other Austrians have discussed.

One framework economists have historically used to understand money's effects on the economy is the equation of exchange. If we let M stand for the money supply, V stand for the velocity of money (or the number of times a given dollar changes hands in a certain period of time, which is also the inverse of the demand to hold money), P be the price level, and Y mean real income, we know that $M \times V$ must equal $P \times Y$. The $MV = PY$ equation simply says that the total amount of money that is spent (M times V, or the money supply times its average turnover) must equal the nominal value of what is sold (P times Y is simply nominal income). $MV = PY$ is an identity, in that it must be true by definition. Therefore, if one variable changes, one or more other variables must change in a way that maintains the identity.

What Selgin and other supporters of the monetary equilibrium approach argue is that maintaining monetary equilibrium is equivalent to maintaining a constant $M \times V$, so any changes in productivity that affect Y must also cause P to move in the opposite direction.[68] Thus, if we maintain monetary equilibrium, economic growth (an increase in Y) will lead to falling prices (a decline in P). Good monetary policy does not try to create a stable price level. Instead, it should aim for monetary equilibrium, thereby allowing the price level to move in response to changes from the real side. Attempting to maintain price-level stability in an economy experiencing productivity gains will lead to inflation, because the price level *should* be falling. This monetary equilibrium perspective can help us understand a point that Rothbard and others made about the 1920s: even though the price level was largely stable, that stability was masking an underlying inflationary boom, because productivity gains of the era should have been driving prices down.[69] This point is crucial to understanding how Austrians might see both monetary policy and economic history differently than other schools of thought, including other largely free-market ones like the Monetarism associated with Milton Friedman and other Chicago School macroeconomists.

Another way to see these differences is through the Austrian emphasis on relative price effects. Whereas much of macroeconomics has seen the costs of inflation and deflation coming from movements in the price level as a whole, the Austrian monetary equilibrium perspective illustrates that the real costs come from distortions of the microeconomic price coordination process.[70] When actors have actual money holdings greater than what they desire and spend those excess balances, they drive up prices. But there is no reason to think that those expenditures will be distributed evenly across the economy. Instead, the effects on prices will be uneven in a manner that depends on who has the excess supply of money and what their preferences are. Some prices will go up by a lot, some by a little. What matters for microeconomic coordination is the price of one good compared to another. As inflation has these uneven effects on prices, some goods rise in relative value and some fall. Those shifting price signals become part of the calculation processes of entrepreneurs and consumers.

This point is even more pronounced when we integrate the Austrian theory of capital into the analysis. Here too Austrians disaggregate the homogeneous "K" of mainstream theory and can thereby better understand the effects of distorted relative prices. If entrepreneurs are fooled by the new set of relative prices caused by the inflation, it can lead them to invest in capital goods they otherwise might not have. Entrepreneurs might turn to whole new projects if they misread inflation-ridden prices. If those prices turn out to be artifacts of inflation, and firms realize the capital they purchased wasn't the right way to spend their money, they will be unable to recoup the full value of that capital.

Recall that capital goods have a limited number of uses. If interest rates are sending false signals about consumer time preferences, they may induce entrepreneurs to invest in capital goods that they later discover were not the correct ones to have used to meet consumer demands. At that point, those specific goods will be worth less than what was paid for them, because they can no longer produce the value they were expected to. The entrepreneurs will have to sell them for a loss, and the buyers will have to invest resources in refitting the capital goods to serve some new, and suboptimal, purpose. Those costs of refitting capital goods, or retraining human capital, are social losses compared to a world without inflation. From this perspective, the Austrian theory of the business cycle can be understood as a particular application of this general story. The boom is a specific pattern of malinvestment induced by inflation having caused an artificially low market rate of interest and intertemporal price distortions. In the end, all of the costs of inflation (and deflation) can be understood as resulting from the relative price effects of monetary disequilibria. This is the sense in which Austrians say there are macroeconomic questions but only microeconomic answers.

Most economic analyses of the costs of inflation look at the problems associated with movements in the price level as a whole, especially unexpected ones. Historically, rising prices were seen as problematic because they meant menus and price tags had to be changed more often and because people might have to make more trips to the bank to get cash. Modern technology has minimized these costs, of course. More recently, the emphasis from the mainstream has been on the costs of anticipating inflation in things like contracts. But here too, it is the changes in the aggregate price level that are at issue. This approach misses the microeconomic effects discussed above. To the degree that those relative price effects cause waste at the microeconomic level and induce people to expend resources to protect themselves against inflation's various effects, the costs of inflation are much larger than normally believed. If that microeconomic discoordination undermines confidence in markets, leading people to prefer the political process as a way to enrich themselves, or allocate resources, then the wastes of inflation will be even greater. To the extent that high levels of inflation undermine the use of money in exchange, hyperinflation can lead to the breakdown of market economies. Because Austrians understand the relative price effects of inflation, they will have a much better and broader accounting of the true costs of inflation and the damage it can inflict. The mainstream's focus on aggregates obscures the real issues at stake.

The differences between the Austrian approach and that of other schools of thought is nicely illustrated in Garrison's *Time and Money*. In that book, he develops what he calls "capital-based macroeconomics," which he contrasts with the "labor-based" macroeconomics of mainstream thought. From Keynesianism's focus on sticky wages through the Phillips Curve tradeoff between inflation and unemployment that defined both Monetarism and the New Classical economics, modern macroeconomics has been focused on the labor market as the link between microeconomics and macroeconomic aggregates. The popular beliefs that inflation can reduce unemployment and that lower unemployment can somehow cause inflation are derived from a labor-based vision of macroeconomics. Garrison contrasted these approaches with the capital-based approach of the Austrians. As we've seen, the heterogeneity of capital, the idea of a capital structure involving stages of production through time, and the need to rely on market prices to engage in monetary calculation in order to allocate that capital are the foundations of the Austrian vision of the market process. The capital structure is also the primary transmission mechanism of monetary disturbances into fluctuations in real variables and the coordination failures they produce.

Garrison introduced a four-quadrant graphical structure that provided a visual tool for explicating the Austrian capital-based approach and contrasting it with other schools of thought, particularly Keynes's approach. By integrating the "Hayekian triangle" (representing the capital structure) with the loanable funds market and a production possibilities frontier that illustrated the tradeoff between consumption and investment, Garrison could show how an increase in savings would generate real economic growth and how excess supplies of money would trigger the unsustainable boom of the Austrian business cycle. He also made explicit the idea of "stage-specific" labor markets, which enabled Austrians to disaggregate "the" labor market and show how shifts in the capital structure would affect wages in different stages of production. The same graphics could be used to explore how fiscal policy might affect the capital structure and growth, which Austrians had not previously explored in any detail. Garrison's diagrams also provided an easy way to contrast the Austrian approach with Keynes's, as the assumptions about the capital structure, the loanable funds market, and the tradeoff between consumption and investment that differentiated the Austrian approach were clearly on display. Other Austrians have expanded Garrison's diagrams and applied them to different macroeconomic problems, including deflation.[71]

In the past decade, Austrian macroeconomics has become more central to the conversation in economics thanks to the financial crisis and Great Recession of the 2000s. During the housing boom, some Austrians had been warning that the economy had features of the boom portion of an Austrian-style cycle. When the bust began in 2006 and 2007, many Austrians quickly offered explanations of the situation using versions of the cycle theory. The expansion of the money supply after 2001 was clearly evident in the drop in the nominal and real federal funds rate, the latter of which was negative for around two years in the middle of the decade. The distinct feature of this cycle was the way in which the excess credit manifested in the housing market rather than in commercial loans, as the canonical Austrian story would suggest. Austrians, and others, pointed out that various government regulations had made housing artificially attractive for both sellers and buyers of mortgages, making that market a major site for the excess credit. Houses do share features with long-lived commercial capital investments, so many of the same Austrian ideas could be applied to housing. In addition, Austrians extended the Rothbardian analysis of the Great Depression to show how poor policy choices in the months and years after the 2008 crash deepened the recession and slowed recovery efforts.[72]

Although Austrians generally opposed the expansion of the Fed's powers and its use of quantitative easing, there has been a healthy debate both among Austrians and between Austrians and the so-called "market monetarists" about the Fed's actions in the fall of 2008, during the depths of the crisis. The market monetarists and most Austrians agree that the Fed had an obligation to prevent a decline in the money supply by making use of the Fed's standard tool of open market operations, as it also should have done but did not do in the early 1930s. It is tempting to think that reducing the money supply would cure the problem of too much money, but once the inflation has happened and prices have adjusted, a subsequent deflation would cause the same problems that any other monetary deflation would cause, regardless of whether it had been preceded by an inflation. The key going forward is to maintain monetary equilibrium. Even though they agree on that important point, the Austrians and the "market monetarists" continue to have a healthy and productive debate about the details of how much the Fed should have done and for how long.

The numerous elements of the crisis and Great Recession that the Austrian theory of the business cycle could explain have put the theory back on the map as an analytic tool within macroeconomics.[73]

From the fairly simple story and narrow focus of the theory of the business cycle that Mises and Hayek developed between the wars, and that Rothbard elaborated in the 1960s, modern Austrian economics now has a richer, more detailed, and more powerful framework for explaining not just the boom and bust of the business cycle but a whole variety of macroeconomic phenomena. These advances have been made as part of an ongoing dialogue with mainstream macroeconomics, with the hope of offering better analyses than do the standard tools. There are still many fascinating phenomena in monetary economics and macroeconomics, from a world of near-zero interest rates to cryptocurrencies like Bitcoin, and the Austrian approach is being applied to all of them.

Austrian Economics
in the 21st Century

It has been almost 150 years since Menger's *Principles* was published, founding what became known as the Austrian School of economics. Those 150 years have seen the school's fortunes rise, then fall, and then revive in the mid-1970s. In the more than 40 years since the start of that revival, the Austrian School has expanded in ways exceeding the heights of its influence early in the 20th century. Austrian-influenced economists have dozens of tenured professorships at a variety of universities worldwide, including ones with PhD programs that are producing the next generations of Austrians. These academic Austrians are publishing their work in major mainstream economics journals, writing books for major publishing houses, and generally engaging the rest of the discipline of economics in the important research questions of the day. Other Austrians, working from think tanks or government offices, are using Austrian ideas to analyze current events and put those analyses into the conversation in the world of public policy. Although the Austrian School is still very much a minority perspective, its adherents have been able to barge their way into a variety of professional conversations by virtue of the high quality of their work.

There are a number of reasons Austrian economists have been more successful in recent years. The key has been the way that modern Austrians have broadened both the set of ideas they are deploying and the scope of the questions they are trying to answer. Austrian economics in the 21st century still rests on the foundation of Menger, Mises, and Hayek, but Austrians have very intentionally found ways to incorporate complementary work from other traditions in economics. The most obvious of these is public choice theory, especially the work of James Buchanan, who won the Nobel Prize in 1986 for his contributions in this area. Buchanan had long been interested in Austrian economics and saw his attempt to explain politics as a form of exchange (which is the essence of public choice) as in line with the catallactic approach of Mises and Hayek. The Austrian and public choice approaches are both interested in the ways in which exchange takes place under specific rules of the game and how likely those rules are to produce desirable or undesirable unintended consequences. This broader combined perspective has enabled younger scholars to bring Austrian ideas to new conversations and has strengthened the influence of Austrian ideas by showing their explanatory power in combination with more widely accepted frameworks.[74]

Even more recently, many younger Austrian scholars have deployed the ideas associated with the Bloomington School of Political Economy that grew out of the work of Vincent and Elinor Ostrom.[75] The work of combining these two perspectives pre-dates Elinor Ostrom's 2009 Nobel Prize, but the increased visibility of her work since then has certainly prompted more integration of the Ostroms' scholarship with modern Austrian insights. The Bloomington emphasis on both the polycentric nature of political decisionmaking and the ways in which communities can develop informal rules and norms for solving many of the problems that interest economists makes that approach a natural partner for Austrians. The Ostroms offer a way to think about how informal rules within smaller, decentralized communities mimic the role of formal property rights and other institutions within larger, more anonymous social groups. Looking at informal norms as an alternative to the formal market process and the large-scale political process gives Austrians a way to use their ideas about decentralized knowledge and emergent orders to address problems that mainstream economists might struggle with. This framework has been especially fruitful in understanding the emergence of self-enforcing contracts and clubs as alternatives to the formal political structure for penalizing and reducing opportunistic behavior.

Finally, post-revival Austrian economists have used this combination of perspectives to explore areas outside the traditional domain of economics. From pirates, to war, to prison gangs, to the social institution of the family, to the large research program that analyzed the recovery from Hurricane Katrina, the modern Austrian School has engaged in what might be termed social theory with economics at its center.[76] The universalizing aspirations of Menger's *Principles* and Mises's *Human Action* have been combined with Hayek's work on the differences between intimate and anonymous social orders to create an analytical framework for rendering a whole variety of human social behavior intelligible. Contemporary Austrian economists are engaged in a project of comparative political economy that offers "analytical narratives," rooted in the microeconomics of Menger, Mises, and Hayek, to explain the puzzles of modern economic and social life. Consistent with the subjectivism and spontaneous order theorizing that characterized Hayek's description of social scientific methodology after World War II, this modern Austrian work starts with the perceptions of actors and explains the patterns of unintended consequences that emerge from the choices individuals make on the basis of their perceived means-ends frameworks and the constraints imposed by both scarcity and the institutional environment. Rather than relying solely on econometric techniques, these analytical narratives embody a pluralistic approach that makes use of a variety of empirical evidence, both qualitative and quantitative, as is appropriate for explaining the particular puzzle in question. Most important, contemporary Austrians are publishing this work through major university and academic presses and in academic journals.

This approach to economics and social science more generally has made it possible for modern Austrians to engage effectively with the disciplines of economics and political science, among others, in areas such as antitrust, monetary policy, business cycles, comparative economic systems, inequality, economic history, and the effectiveness of alternative political institutions. Austrians and Austrian-influenced scholars are making significant contributions in all of these areas, as well as others, in ways that the school has not done since its zenith between the wars. With multiple PhD programs producing scholars trained in both Austrian economics and the related traditions it is often combined with, the prospects for continued expansion of both the range of Austrian scholarship and its influence in contemporary social science seem brighter than ever.

The Austrian School emerged out of the Marginal Revolution that founded modern neoclassical economics. The first few generations of Austrian economists made foundational contributions that remain part of the field today. Even as their influence was eclipsed by a combination of world events and changes in the intellectual climate during the middle of the 20th century, their ideas survived. As the failures of both socialism and Keynesianism became clear in the 1970s, many of the Austrians' ideas that had been rejected decades earlier gained new life, especially in the wake of Hayek's Nobel Prize in 1974. The resilience of those ideas is suggestive of their explanatory power, but in the decades that followed the 1970s, those ideas had to be refreshed, critically assessed, and then presented in ways relevant to a discipline that was very different from the one it was when the Austrian School was at either its height or its depths. The evidence so far suggests that the post-revival generation of Austrian economists have undertaken that project successfully: modern Austrian economics is a substantively different, although still recognizable, intellectual endeavor from what it used to be and is showing numerous signs of growth and increasing influence. Studying the long history of Austrian economics is not an exercise in historical curiosity. Rather, it is the foundation necessary for grappling with the most important ideas in contemporary political economy and then applying those ideas to the pressing puzzles of economic and social life in the modern world.

Notes

Chapter 1

1. Robert Nozick, *Anarchy, State, and Utopia* (New York: Basic Books, 1974).

2. Israel Kirzner, *Competition and Entrepreneurship* (Chicago: University of Chicago Press, 1973).

3. Carl Menger, *Principles of Economics* (New York: New York University Press, 1981), p. 108.

4. Carl Menger, *Investigations into the Method of the Social Sciences with Special Reference to Economics* (New York: New York University Press, 1985), p. 146.

Chapter 2

5. For a more contemporary Austrian treatment of these issues, see James M. Buchanan, *Cost and Choice* (Chicago: University of Chicago Press, 1969).

6. This phrase is taken from Ludwig Lachmann's short book on the Austrian theory of capital, *Capital and its Structure* (Kansas City, MO: Sheed Andrews and McMeel, 1978).

7. The most thorough discussion of this approach to supply and demand can be found in Murray Rothbard, *Man, Economy, and State* (Los Angeles: Nash Publishing, 1962), pp. 1–66.

Chapter 3

8. One of the best treatments of the differences among the three thinkers at the heart of the Marginal Revolution is William Jaffe, "Menger, Jevons and Walras De-Homogenized," *Economic Inquiry* 14 (1976): 511–24.

9. See also Carl Menger, "On the Origin of Money," *Economic Journal* 2 (1892): 239–55.

10. F. A. Hayek, "The Results of Human Action but Not of Human Design," in F. A. Hayek, *Studies in Politics, Philosophy, and Economics* (Chicago: University of Chicago Press, 1967), pp. 96–105.

11. Adam Smith, *An Inquiry into the Nature and Causes of the Wealth of Nations*, ed. Edwin Cannan, 1904 ed. (Chicago: University of Chicago Press, 1976), p. 477.

12. On the relationship of the Scots to the Austrians, see Steven Horwitz, "From Smith to Menger to Hayek: Liberalism in the Spontaneous Order Tradition," *The Independent Review* 6 (2001): 81–97.

Chapter 4

13. Ludwig von Mises, *Human Action: A Treatise on Economics* (Chicago: Henry Regnery, 1966), p. 405.

14. For a more detailed discussion, see Lawrence White's "Introduction to the New York University Press Edition" in Menger, *Investigations into the Method of the Social Sciences with Special Reference to Economics* (New York: New York University Press, 1985).

15. For an overview of the issues in the *methodenstreit*, see Samuel Bostaph, "The Methodological Debate Between Carl Menger and the German Historical School," *Atlantic Economic Journal* 6 (September 1978): 3–16.

16. The following discussion borrows heavily from Steven Horwitz, "The Empirics of Austrian Economics," *Cato Unbound* (September 5, 2012), https://www.cato-unbound.org/2012/09/05/steven-horwitz/empirics-austrian-economics.

17. Mises, *Human Action: A Treatise on Economics*, p. 236.

18. Stephen T. Ziliak and Deirdre N. McCloskey, *The Cult of Statistical Significance: How the Standard Error Costs Us Jobs, Justice and Lives* (Ann Arbor: University of Michigan Press, 2008).

Chapter 5

19. For more on the role of monetary calculation, see Mises, *Human Action: A Treatise on Economics*, pp. 200–31; Ludwig von Mises, "Profit and Loss," in *Planning for Freedom: Let the Market System Work* (Indianapolis: Liberty Fund Press, 2008), pp. 143–72; Peter Boettke, "Economic Calculation: The Austrian Contribution to Political Economy," in *Calculation and Coordination* (New York: Routledge, 2001), pp. 29–46; and Steven Horwitz, "Monetary Calculation and the Unintended Extended Order: The Misesian Microfoundations of the Hayekian Great Society," *Review of Austrian Economics* 17 (2004): 307–21.

20. See the discussion in Lachmann's *Capital and its Structure*, pp. 1–19.

21. Or, to use Peter Boettke's analogy: for Austrians, capital is better thought of as pieces of a Lego set than as hunks of malleable Play-Doh.

22. Menger, *Principles of Economics*, pp. 55–67.

Chapter 6

23. Ludwig von Mises, "Economic Calculation in the Socialist Commonwealth," in *Collectivist Economic Planning*, ed. F. A. Hayek (Clifton, NJ: Augustus M. Kelley, 1975), pp. 87–130; Ludwig von Mises, *Socialism: An Economic and Sociological Analysis* (Indianapolis, IN: Liberty Press, 1981).

24. Mises, "Economic Calculation in the Socialist Commonwealth," in *Collectivist Economic Planning*, p. 102.

25. Oskar Lange, "On the Economic Theory of Socialism," in *On the Economic Theory of Socialism*, ed. Benjamin Lippincott (New York: McGraw-Hill, 1964).

26. See Hayek's three articles on economic calculation, all of which can be found in his *Individualism and Economic Order* (Chicago: University of Chicago Press, 1948): "The Nature and History of the Problem," "The Present State of the Debate," and "The Competitive Solution."

27. See, in particular, F. A. Hayek's most famous essay, "The Use of Knowledge in Society," *The American Economic Review* 35 (4):519–30; the 1945 essay was reprinted in Hayek, *Individualism and Economic Order.*

28. Don Lavoie, *Rivalry and Central Planning: The Socialist Calculation Debate Reconsidered* (Cambridge, MA: Cambridge University Press, 1985).

29. Robert Heilbroner, "The Triumph of Capitalism," *The New Yorker*, January 23, 1989, p. 98.

Chapter 7

30. See Ludwig von Mises, *The Theory of Money and Credit* (Indianapolis, IN: Liberty Press, 1980) and F. A. Hayek, *Monetary Theory and the Trade Cycle* (Clifton, NJ: Augustus M. Kelley, 1966).

31. Knut Wicksell, *Interest and Prices* (Auburn, AL: The Ludwig von Mises Institute, 2007).

32. See the discussion in Mises, *The Theory of Money and Credit*, chap. 19.

33. Or, as the Fed has done since 2008, when the central bank lowers the interest rate it pays banks to hold reserves, making lending those reserves out marginally more attractive.

34. Mises, *Human Action: A Treatise on Economics*, p. 427.

35. John Maynard Keynes, *A Treatise on Money* (London: Macmillan and Company, 1930).

36. F. A. Hayek, "Reflections on the Pure Theory of Money of Mr. J. M. Keynes," *Economica* 35 (February 1932): 22–44, reprinted in *The Collected Works of F. A. Hayek, Vol. 9: Contra Keynes and Cambridge*, ed. Bruce Caldwell (Chicago: University of Chicago Press, 1995).

37. John Maynard Keynes, *The General Theory of Employment, Interest, and Money* (New York: Harcourt, Brace and Company, 1936).

38. See Keynes, *The General Theory of Employment, Interest, and Money*. These ideas still form the basic model in many introductory macroeconomics courses, known as the "Keynesian Cross."

39. On the contrast between Keynes and the Austrians discussed in this section, see Steven Horwitz, *Microfoundations and Macroeconomics: An Austrian Perspective* (New York: Routledge, 2000), pp. 86–90, and Roger Garrison, *Time and Money: The Macroeconomics of Capital Structure* (New York: Routledge, 2001), chap. 7.

40. The core ideas of the Hayek-Keynes debate, in terms of both theory and policy, are nicely captured in the John Papola and Russ Roberts music videos about these issues. See "Fear the Boom and Bust," https://www.youtube.com/watch?v=d0nERTFo-Sk, and "Fight of the Century," https://www.youtube.com/watch?v=GTQnarzmTOc.

41. The following section draws from Steven Horwitz, "Contrasting Concepts of Capital: Yet Another Look at the Hayek-Keynes Debate," *Journal of Private Enterprise* 27 (2011): 9–27.

42. For more on the Austrian view of the Great Depression, see Murray Rothbard, *America's Great Depression,* 5th ed. (Auburn, AL: The Ludwig von Mises Institute, 2000), and Steven Horwitz, "Great Apprehensions, Prolonged Depression: Gauti Eggertsson on the 1930s," *Econ Journal Watch* 6 (2009): 313–36. For a discussion written for a broader audience that relies on many Austrian ideas, see Lawrence Reed, *Great Myths of the Great Depression* (Midland, MI: Mackinac Center for Public Policy, 2012), https://fee.org/media/16865/great_myths_of_the_great_depression_2016.pdf.

43. F. A. Hayek, *The Pure Theory of Capital* (Chicago: University of Chicago Press, 1941).

Chapter 8

44. The best overview of Hayek's intellectual project and its transformation during this period is Bruce Caldwell, *Hayek's Challenge* (Chicago: University of Chicago Press, 2004).

45. F. A. Hayek, "Economics and Knowledge," *Economica IV* (1937): 33–54, reprinted in Hayek, *Individualism and Economic Order*, p. 42.

46. Hayek, "Economics and Knowledge," reprinted in Hayek, *Individualism and Economic Order*, p. 45.

47. Hayek, "The Use of Knowledge in Society."

48. Hayek, "The Use of Knowledge in Society," in *Individualism and Economic Order*, p. 79.

49. Hayek, "The Use of Knowledge in Society," in *Individualism and Economic Order*, pp. 80, 83.

50. See Horwitz, "Monetary Calculation and the Unintended Extended Order."

51. F. A. Hayek, *The Counter-Revolution of Science* (Indianapolis, IN: Liberty Press, 1952).

52. Hayek, *The Counter-Revolution of Science*, p. 44.

53. Hayek, *The Counter-Revolution of Science*, chap. 4.

Chapter 9

54. The story of the modern Austrian revival is best told in Karen Vaughn, *Austrian Economics in America* (Cambridge, MA: Cambridge University Press, 1994).

55. F. A. Hayek, "The Meaning of Competition," Stafford Little Lecture delivered at Princeton University (1946), reprinted in Hayek, *Individualism and Economic Order*.

56. Hayek, "The Meaning of Competition," reprinted in Hayek, *Individualism and Economic Order*, p. 96.

57. Hayek, "The Meaning of Competition," reprinted in Hayek, *Individualism and Economic Order*, p. 97; italics in the original.

58. Kirzner, *Competition and Entrepreneurship*.

59. See, for example, Israel Kirzner, *Discovery, Capitalism, and Distributive Justice* (New York: Blackwell, 1989), chap. 2.

60 F. A. Hayek, "Competition as a Discovery Procedure," in *New Studies in Politics, Philosophy, Economics and the History of Ideas* (Chicago: University of Chicago Press, 1978).

61. For an earlier Austrian treatment of this point, see Dominick T. Armentano, *Antitrust and Monopoly: Anatomy of a Policy Failure*, 2nd ed. (New York: Holmes and Meier, 1990).

62. Adam Thierer, *Permissionless Innovation: The Continuing Case for Comprehensive Technological Freedom*, 2nd ed. (Arlington, VA: The Mercatus Center at George Mason University, 2016).

Chapter 10

63. Rothbard, *America's Great Depression*.

64. Lawrence H. White, *Free Banking in Britain* (Cambridge: Cambridge University Press, 1984); George Selgin, *The Theory of Free Banking Money Supply*

Under Competitive Note Issue (Totowa, NJ: Rowman and Littlefield, 1988); Horwitz, *Microfoundations and Macroeconomics*; Garrison, *Time and Money*.

65. See also Steven Horwitz, "Capital Theory, Inflation, and Deflation: The Austrians and Monetary Disequilibrium Theory Compared," *Journal of the History of Economic Thought* 18 (1996): 287–308.

66. Some Austrian economists (such as Rothbard in *Man, Economy, and State* [1962]) have argued that fractional reserve banking will not keep investment and saving coordinated and that a 100 percent reserve requirement is needed. This view depends on a misunderstanding of the nature of the demand for bank money and its relationship to savings, and it has been supplanted by the more modern view described here. For more on this issue, see Selgin, *The Theory of Free Banking Money Supply Under Competitive Note Issue.*

67. George Selgin, *Less than Zero: The Case for a Falling Price Level in a Growing Economy*, Hobart Paper #132 (London: The Institute of Economic Affairs, 1997).

68. Hayek also made this argument in 1935. See his *Prices and Production*, 2nd ed. (New York: Augustus M. Kelley, 1967).

69. See Rothbard, *America's Great Depression*, pp. 169–70.

70. See Horwitz, *Microfoundations and Macroeconomics*, chap. 4.

71. Interested readers should consult Garrison's fantastic PowerPoint slides that illustrate much of this argument, https://www.auburn.edu/~garriro/ppsus.htm.

72. See, among others, Roger Koppl, *From Crisis to Confidence: Macroeconomics after the Crash* (London: The Institute of Economic Affairs, 2014) and Steven Horwitz, "The Financial Crisis in the United States" in *Oxford Handbook of Austrian Economics*, ed. Peter J. Boettke and Christopher Coyne (New York: Oxford University Press, 2015), pp. 729–48.

73. See the essays in David Beckworth, ed., *Boom and Bust Banking: The Causes and Cures of the Great Recession* (Oakland, CA: The Independent Institute, 2012).

Chapter 11

74. See Peter J. Boettke and Alain Marciano, "The Past, Present, and Future of Virginia Political Economy," *Public Choice* 163 (2015): 53–65.

75. See Paul Dragos Aligica and Peter J. Boettke, *Challenging Institutional Analysis and Development: The Bloomington School* (New York: Routledge, 2009).

76. Peter Leeson, *The Invisible Hook* (Princeton: Princeton University Press, 2009); Christopher Coyne, *After War: The Political Economy of Exporting Democracy* (Stanford: Stanford University Press, 2007); David Skarbek, *The Social Order of the Underworld: How Prison Gangs Govern the American Penal System* (New York: Oxford University Press, 2014); and Steven Horwitz, *Hayek's Modern Family: Classical Liberalism and the Evolution of Social Institutions* (New York: Palgrave, 2015). The large research project on Hurricane Katrina can be found here, along with citations to the relevant literature: https://www.mercatus.org/tags/disaster-recovery#1.

Further Reading

Carl Menger, *Principles of Economics*, 1871. This is where it all began, as Menger's *Principles* was the founding text of what became known as the Austrian School. It remains both readable to the nonspecialist and a continuing source of insights to those who are decades deep in the tradition. One of the great things about the revival in Austrian economics of the past few decades is how much the tradition has recovered the insights about knowledge, uncertainty, and disequilibrium processes that Menger glimpsed at the start.

F. A. Hayek, *Individualism and Economic Order*, 1948. This book and the Mises book that follows belong together. They were published at almost the same time, and they were the two books most responsible for the revival of Austrian economics that began in earnest 25 years later. The Hayek book is a collection of his academic articles from the 1930s and 1940s that includes not just the three papers on socialist calculation, but also the three papers on knowledge and competition that provide the defining insights for the past 40 years of Austrian economics. These papers are at the core of modern Austrian economics.

Ludwig von Mises, *Human Action*, 1949. Mises's book, of course, is the treatise and intellectual tour de force that has become the near-encyclopedic touchstone for the modern Austrian school. It offers everything from the philosophical foundations of economics, to the place of economics in the world of ideas, to coverage of the core principles of the discipline. While the Hayek book focused on more narrow, but crucial, debates in economics, Mises's book was written for the ages as a statement about the nature of economics. In that way, the Hayek and Mises books make an ideal pair.

Israel Kirzner, *Competition and Entrepreneurship*, 1973. If the Hayek and Mises books set the stage for the revival, Kirzner's work—and this book in particular—showed how the ideas in those volumes could be put to work in the context of modern economics. Not only is Kirzner's book important for developing the central roles of competition and entrepreneurship in the Austrian vision, it also demonstrated how the Austrian theory differed from the then-current work on the topics in the mainstream of the discipline. The book is a model of scholarly engagement between Austrians and neoclassical economics that enabled Austrian ideas to be taken seriously by the broader profession.

Index

Note: Page numbers with "n" indicate endnotes.

About the Author

Steven Horwitz is the Distinguished Professor of Free Enterprise in the Department of Economics at Ball State University in Muncie, Indiana. A member of the Mont Pelerin Society, he has a PhD in economics from George Mason University and an AB in economics and philosophy from the University of Michigan.

Horwitz is the author of *Monetary Evolution, Free Banking, and Economic Order* (Westview, 1992), *Microfoundations and Macroeconomics: An Austrian Perspective* (Routledge, 2000), and *Hayek's Modern Family: Classical Liberalism and the Evolution of Social Institutions* (Palgrave Macmillan, 2015). He has written extensively on Austrian economics, Hayekian political economy, monetary theory and history, and American economic history. His work has been published in professional journals such as *History of Political Economy*, the *Southern Economic Journal*, and the *Cambridge Journal of Economics*.

Horwitz is also an affiliated senior scholar at the Mercatus Center at George Mason University in Arlington, Virginia; a senior fellow at the Fraser Institute in Canada; and a distinguished scholar at the Foundation for Economic Education. He has done public policy research for the Mercatus Center, the Heartland Institute, and the Cato Institute, and he has been a guest on several radio and cable TV shows. Horwitz has spoken to professional, student, policymaker, and general audiences throughout North America, as well as in Asia, Europe, and South America.

Prior to Ball State, he taught for 28 years at St. Lawrence University in New York, where he is Professor of Economics Emeritus.

Libertarianism.org

Liberty. It's a simple idea and the linchpin of a complex system of values and practices: justice, prosperity, responsibility, toleration, cooperation, and peace. Many people believe that liberty is the core political value of modern civilization itself, the one that gives substance and form to all the other values of social life. They're called libertarians.

Libertarianism.org is the Cato Institute's treasury of resources about the theory and history of liberty. The book you're holding is a small part of what Libertarianism.org has to offer. In addition to hosting classic texts by historical libertarian figures and original articles from modern-day thinkers, Libertarianism.org publishes podcasts, videos, online introductory courses, and books on a variety of topics within the libertarian tradition.

Cato Institute

Founded in 1977, the Cato Institute is a public policy research foundation dedicated to broadening the parameters of policy debate to allow consideration of more options that are consistent with the principles of limited government, individual liberty, and peace. To that end, the Institute strives to achieve greater involvement of the intelligent, concerned lay public in questions of policy and the proper role of government.

The Institute is named for *Cato's Letters*, libertarian pamphlets that were widely read in the American Colonies in the early 18th century and played a major role in laying the philosophical foundation for the American Revolution.

Despite the achievement of the nation's Founders, today virtually no aspect of life is free from government encroachment. A pervasive intolerance for individual rights is shown by government's arbitrary intrusions into private economic transactions and its disregard for civil liberties. And while freedom around the globe has notably increased in the past several decades, many countries have moved in the opposite direction, and most governments still do not respect or safeguard the wide range of civil and economic liberties.

To address those issues, the Cato Institute undertakes an extensive publications program on the complete spectrum of policy issues. Books, monographs, and shorter studies are commissioned to examine the federal budget, Social Security, regulation, military spending, international trade, and myriad other issues. Major policy conferences are held throughout the year, from which papers are published thrice yearly in the *Cato Journal*. The Institute also publishes the quarterly magazine *Regulation*.

In order to maintain its independence, the Cato Institute accepts no government funding. Contributions are received from foundations, corporations, and individuals, and other revenue is generated from the sale of publications. The Institute is a nonprofit, tax-exempt, educational foundation under Section 501(c)3 of the Internal Revenue Code.

CATO INSTITUTE
1000 Massachusetts Avenue, NW
Washington, DC 20001
www.cato.org

Lightning Source UK Ltd.
Milton Keynes UK
UKHW040417121220
374897UK00005BA/883